The Right Word!

The
Right

How to Say
What You
Really
Mean

Word!

Jan Venolia

Author of *Write Right!* and *Rewrite Right!*

Ten Speed Press
<small>Berkeley • Toronto</small>

Ten Speed Press
Box 7123
Berkeley, California 94707
www.tenspeed.com

Distributed in Australia by Simon & Schuster Australia, in Canada by Ten Speed Press Canada, in New Zealand by Southern Publishers Group, in South Africa by Real Books, and in the United Kingdom and Europe by Airlift Book Company.

Cover design by Paul Kepple
Book design by Tasha Hall
Illustrations by Andrea Arden Penn

Library of Congress Cataloging-in-Publication Data

Venolia, Jan.

The right word! : how to say what you really mean / Jan Venolia ; illustrations by Andrea Arden Penn.

p. cm.

Includes bibliographical references and index.

ISBN 1-58008-507-5 (pbk.)

1. English language—Usage—Dictionaries. I. Title.

PE1464 .V46 2003

428'.003—dc21

2003009462

Printed in Canada
First printing, this edition, 2003

1 2 3 4 5 6 7 8 9 10 — 08 07 06 05 04 03

> We are talking about tools and carpentry, about words and style, . . . but as we move along, you'd do well to remember that we are also talking about magic.
> —Stephen King
>
> Need magic? Turn the page.
> —Jan Venolia

Contents

A Few Words about Words

Why this book? Why now? Because we're having an epidemic of wrong-worditis. It permeates schools, surfaces in boardrooms, and infiltrates the airwaves. It echoes through the halls of Congress and issues from the White House.

Surely, you may say, using wrong words is far down the list of problems that demand our attention. But look at it this way: Communication is fundamental to human interaction; words are crucial to communication. Whether we're talking about jobs, education, community activism, or love affairs, human interaction is what's happening. It's more likely to go well if we use the right words.

> Language is everything and everywhere; it's
> what lets us have anything to do with one
> another.—David Foster Wallace

Wrong words get in the way of "having anything to do with one another." They mislead and occasionally make us look foolish, as the following sentences show. (I didn't make them up.)

She was naked from the waste down.

The ordinance reigned in adult-oriented establishments.

You're a real suppository of information.

If you're wondering which of those words are "wrong," keep reading. Or maybe you know which are wrong but you wonder why the fuss; you were, after all, able to figure out what was meant. In either case, this book is for you.

The Right Word! explains the difference between *waste* and *waist*, *reign in* and *rein in*. (I hope you already know the difference between a suppository and a repository.) As for the question, Does it matter? You bet it does. Readers or listeners shouldn't have to struggle to understand what you're saying. Every time you impede comprehension or generate fogginess, you sabotage your reason for communicating. What's more, unclear communication can make you look sloppy or uneducated; it suggests that you have limitations elsewhere as well.

What's going on here? How did we arrive at such a place? Much of the time, communication reaches the brain through the ear instead of the eye. When a newscaster or commentator uses a word we don't know, our brains translate the unfamiliar sound into a familiar one. In the process, the right word becomes a near miss; "windshield factor" and "Cadillac converter" (i.e., *windchill factor* and *catalytic converter*) propagate like rabbits.

But there's more to wrong words than mispronunciation and incorrect definitions. To communicate well, you need to convey what you have in mind without being verbose or stilted; you should know how words are used and be sensitive to their overtones. Take the words *exceptional* and *abnormal*. Though both indicate deviation from a norm, try telling a friend that his child is *abnormal,* and you'll quickly learn there's a difference between the two. As the *UPI Stylebook* states, "A *burro* is an ass. A *burrow* is a hole in the ground. . . . You are expected to know the difference."

Who decides which words are "right" and which are "wrong"? Language, after all, changes. The English we speak is not the English of Shakespeare's time. Should we resist such change or embrace it?

According to some linguists, correct usage is whatever language is spoken; change is not only natural but inevitable. These linguists are usually called "descriptivists," but I'm inclined to call them the "whatever" school of thought. It's as if correctness is determined by taking a poll.

Those who are more apt to stick with rules (at least the rules that add precision and clarity) are called "prescriptivists." The battleground between the two camps is muddy and much trodden.

I guess my own position is already obvious. Even though I believe flexibility is one of the strengths of our language, I see three hazards in the "whatever" approach.

1. Nothing is communicated.

2. The wrong thing is communicated.

3. Vagueness and uncertainty take over.

The objective of *The Right Word!* is to provide you with the tools to avoid all three.

Author Patricia O'Conner (*Woe Is I*) compares the give-and-take of language to warfare: "A word bravely soldiers on for years, until one day it falls face down in the trenches, its original meaning a casualty of misuse." She cites the example of *unique*, a word that originally meant one of a kind but is gradually changing to mean unusual.

You'll find me in the trenches, working with other lovers of the language to keep *unique* from being watered down to "unusual" as its meaning and noo-kyuh-ler from being an acceptable pronunciation of *nuclear*. When people have a unique experience, I want them to have powerful words to describe it. And if someone has a finger on the nuclear button, I want that person to understand the word well enough to know how to pronounce it (noo-klee-er).

> If language is not correct, then what is said is not what is meant; if what is said is not what is meant, then what must be done remains undone; if this remains undone, morals and art will deteriorate; if justice goes astray, the people will stand about in helpless confusion. Hence, there must be no arbitrariness in what is said. This matters above everything.—Confucius

No more standing about in helpless confusion—*The Right Word!* will help you say what you really mean. The first section, OUR LINGUISTIC LEGACY, takes as its premise that the more you know about the English language, the more skilled you will be in using it. To that end, I explore some related subjects:

- word roots and formation
- searching for synonyms
- toxic English
- English on the Internet

The second section, TRICKY WORDS AND HANDY PHRASES, provides a road map around the linguistic booby traps and verbal gaffes that are common in our language. It sorts out the *affects* and *effects*, the *prostrate* and *prostate* that bamboozle many writers. My approach to these questions of usage is from an American perspective; the differences between American and British usage are extensive and are well covered elsewhere.

This section also includes foreign phrases and out-of-the-ordinary words that will stretch your vocabulary, making it more useful in a variety of situations. You might want to create your own tricky words list to speed that process and to reinforce how to use certain important words.

Following the A-to-Z list are "What Do They Mean When They Say . . . ," which throws light on such expressions as *Pyrrhic victory* and *Pandora's box*, and "Figures of Speech," which provides some fancy names for, well, figures of speech. You aren't sure what a figure of speech is? Turn to p. 151 and find out.

ADDITIONAL RESOURCES identifies books, periodicals, and websites that supplement the information presented in these pages.

The Right Word! completes a trilogy on word-related subjects. The first two volumes, *Write Right!* and *Rewrite Right!*, cover grammar, punctuation, writing style, and revision. They help you put words together effectively and concisely. Helping you choose which words to put together is the subject of this book.

> . . . some people still want to use the language well. They want to write effectively; they want to speak effectively. They want their language to be graceful at times and powerful at times. They want to understand how to use words well, how to manipulate sentences, and how to move about in the language without seeming to flail. . . . [T]hey want to use the language deftly so that it's fit for their purposes.—Bryan A. Garner

Since expanding your vocabulary is one of my objectives in helping you "use the language well," I may occasionally use words you don't know. If you encounter such a word, first check to see if it appears in the A-to-Z list. If it's not there, look the word up in your dictionary. Doing so will reinforce the techniques for finding and using the right words.

You can read this book from cover to cover or only dip into it when you need help with particular words. Either way, be sure to linger and enjoy the process.

Look for the jesters who point out entertaining information under the headings Word Play, Word Roots, and Odds & Ends.

As you explore *The Right Word!*, you will discover that our language is indeed full of treasures and delights.

English speakers have absorbed words from around the globe.

Our Linguistic Legacy

When we count our blessings, seldom do we include the alphabet in our litany of things to be thankful for. But just try to imagine life without it. Galileo celebrated this "arrangement of two dozen little signs upon paper" as one of the most stupendous inventions of the human mind. The dictionaries, phone books, and filing systems that we take for granted would be impossible without the alphabet.

Pictograms, the earliest form of writing, consisted of marks to represent tangible objects (say, an ox) or business transactions (I give you two goats, you give me one ox). When letters representing *sounds* replaced pictograms, writing became far more useful. No longer restricted to pictorial representations, words could refer to abstract concepts like bravery. And written words now allowed people to communicate ideas even when they were separated by distance and time.

From the standpoint of convenience alone, the alphabet was an important advance. Consider the computer keyboard, that compact little device you can tuck under one arm. Bill Bryson (author of *The Mother Tongue* and *A Dictionary of Troublesome Words*) estimates that a keyboard able to accommodate

Chinese ideographs would have to be the size of two Ping-Pong tables. Not too handy.

So let's take a look at our linguistic legacy. Poet John Ciardi called written words "small fossil poems written by the race itself." In the paragraphs that follow, we'll go on a quick archaeological dig to see what we can learn about these fossils.

Rooting Around

Where do English words come from? Only about 2 percent originated in England. Words originating in the Americas account for another small percentage, although they include some of our more colorful words: *muckrake, papoose, pothole, squash.* (See "Where Do We Get Our Words?" p. 5.) Although English is classified as a Germanic language, English speakers have absorbed more words from other languages than they have from German, enthusiastically enriching their vocabularies with words from around the globe. Once arrived, these words often evolved until only a scholar can see, for example, the blend of German, Old English, Middle Dutch, and Latin that turned *peisc* into *fish.*

Though I'm neither archaeologist nor word scholar, I do enjoy learning about the roots of words. Thus, when I recently used the word *camouflage,* I wondered about its origin. The *American Heritage Dictionary (AHD)* provided some surprising information. Starting with the French word *camoufler,* meaning to disguise, *AHD* traces the word back to *camouflet* (smoke blown into someone's nose), which has roots in *chault mouflet,* meaning hot face, which, in turn, came from *Muffel,* a German word for snout or mouth. Henceforth, I will use *camouflage* with new respect. Smoke blown into someone's nose, hot face, snout—who would have guessed!

The evolution of words has been likened to the way living beings are born, grow, reproduce, age, and sometimes become extinct. A word like *eximious* (excellent) disappears, while *exasperate* lives on unchanged.

> No dictionary of a living tongue can ever be perfect, since while it is hastening to publication, some words are budding, and some are fading away.—Samuel Johnson

Estimates of how many "budding words" make their way into the language each year range from 5,000 (word maven Richard Lederer) to 20,000 *(New York Times)*. But don't be intimidated by such numbers. One lexicographer, G. H. McKnight, determined that 43 words account for one-quarter of the words in almost any sample of written English. In other words, a few words carry much of the load for us.

Yet another lexicographer, John McWhorter, says that although 99 percent of the words in the *Oxford English Dictionary* are derived from other languages, the remaining 1 percent (of Old English origin) constitute 62 percent of the words we use. Examples he cites include *but, father, love, fight, to, will, and, should, not,* and *from.* Wordplay expert Willard Espy claims that one-fourth of our verbal discourse consists of a mere 17 words: *and, be, have, it, of, the, to, will, you, I, a, on, that, in, we, for,* and *us.* This is not to suggest that you could write great English if you used only McKnight's 43 words or

Espy's 17 or McWhorter's 1 percent, but rather that relatively few words provide the backbone of our mother tongue.*

The average English-speaking adult has a vocabulary of 30,000 to 60,000 words. A highly literate person's could extend to 100,000 words. Yet roughly a million English words have been identified. How is it that we don't use nine-tenths of the existing English language? Because it consists largely of the jargon of specialists. They speak to each other with words that few of us understand or need.

Even so, the jargon of one such area of specialization—science and technology—spills over into everyday language. It provides us with a rich source of new words: *cyberspace*, *hemoglobin*, *genome*, *decibel*, *fractal*—even the word *technology* itself.

What are some other sources of words? Error is responsible for a large number. Mistakes are perpetuated when words are copied or transcribed from speech (*buttonhold* became *buttonhole*, *sweetard* became *sweetheart*). The inability to pronounce a word created so many new words that it earned its own label: Hobson-Jobson. A Hobson-Jobson turns a difficult word or phrase into something more tractable (or perhaps less offensive). By that route, a Texas river that French trappers had named Purgatoire became the Picketwire, and the Malay word *kampong* became the English word *compound*. The term Hobson-Jobson is itself a Hobson-Jobson, an alteration of the Arabic ritual cry of mourning for Husan and Husein, Muhammad's grandsons who were killed in battle.

*To the alert reader who charges me with creating a mixed metaphor, I plead guilty. While I'm completely serious in wanting to help people improve how they use language, I'm equally dedicated to having fun in the process. The Word Play examples throughout this book indicate that I am only one in an army of such word devotees.

WORD ROOTS **Where Do We Get Our Words?**

powwow, chipmunk, hominy, possum: *Algonquin*

alcohol, alfalfa, algebra: *Arabic*

ketchup, kowtow: *Chinese*

chaise, cliché, etiquette, limousine, milieu: *French*

delicatessen, kindergarten, ouch, wanderlust: *German*

blarney, limerick, plaid, slogan, smithereen: *Irish*

broccoli, ghetto, influenza, manifesto, and a host of musical terms (libretto, opera, presto): *Italian*

yen, honcho, tsunami: *Japanese*

chaparral, cork, junta, marijuana, molasses: *Spanish*

bagel, kibitz, lox, schmaltz: *Yiddish*

Other words arise from a process called "back formation." For instance, the verb *diagnose* came from the noun *diagnosis*, *surveil* from *surveillance*, and *enthuse* from *enthusiasm*. Linguists are sometimes slow to accept such back-formed words, especially if they just add clutter. For example, *orientate* (from *orientation*) is considered a clumsy alternative to the existing verb *orient*, and *administrate* a poor choice when *administer* is already available. *Diagnose*, on the other hand, has made it all the way to acceptability.

The phenomenon of "semantic drift," though it doesn't create new words, does gradually produce new meanings for existing words. These are sometimes quite contrary to the original meaning. *Brave* once implied cowardice (which *bravado* still suggests), and *silly*, having started out as happy or blessed, spent some time meaning pitiable, on its way to the present meaning of lacking good sense. The word *tell* originally meant to count (hence, bank *teller*).

The parentage of some words is unknown (*dog*, *put*, *fun*), but others can be traced to specific individuals. Shakespeare stands out among word makers; about one-tenth of his roughly 18,000 words had never been seen before (*critical*, *majestic*, *dwindle*, *lonely*, *obscene*). Ben Jonson gave us *damp*, *strenuous*, and *defunct*, and Sir Thomas More was the source of *absurdity* and *exact*.

We sometimes create new words by combining two existing words into a compound word: *airport*, *rubberneck*, *skyscraper*. We shorten others to simplify them: *fax* from *facsimile*, *email* from *electronic mail*, and *blog* from *web log*. By adding a suffix to the noun *child*, we give birth to the adjective *childlike*. When we shift letters from one word to an adjoining word (a process called *nunnciation*), *an ewt* (a variety of salamander) becomes *a newt* and *a napron* becomes *an apron*.

Lewis Carroll combined *chuckle* and *snort* into *chortle* and called his creation a *portmanteau word*, an allusion to the briefcase with two compartments. *Agitprop*, from *agitation* and *propaganda* is such a two-for-one word.

> *The good news about our unruly, intensely democratic way of making and using words is that . . . our language [is] one of the most energetic, flexible, and just plain fun tongues on Earth.*—Evan Morris

The idea that we can have fun with words seems to have been part of our "hard wiring" for thousands of years. Even as written language was being used for serious purposes, someone must have noticed that rearranging the letters of a word creates a new word; thus was born the anagram.

An **anagram** is the rearrangement of all letters in a word to create a new word.

conversation = voices rant on

telegraph = great help

revolution = to love ruin

punishment = nine thumps

endearments = tender names

a stitch in time saves nine = this is meant as incentive

William Shakespeare = We all make his praise

Palindromes have probably been around since the third century B.C., challenging word addicts to create ever better sentences that read the same in both directions. Thanks to devoted word lovers, we have puns, rebuses, and pangrams (which you'll find illustrated in these pages). For some, the day does not begin until a crossword puzzle has been conquered (or at least tackled); for others, a day is incomplete unless a pun has been slipped into the conversation.

Despite the low esteem in which puns seem to be held, whole communities can become infected by them. On a trip through the Southwest, I observed an outbreak of puns in store names and signs along the highway. Blazing Paddles (a river outfitter); Cram-a-lot (a garbage dumpster); and The Garden of Weedin' (a large vegetable patch). Even the state of Utah fell victim to the contagion with its license plate: Greatest Snow on Earth.

> *Puns are good, bad, and indifferent, and only those who lack the wit to make them are unaware of the fact.*—H. W. Fowler

Honey, Somebody Shrunk the Kids' Vocabulary

English can be likened to a crazy quilt. It has grown from verbal bits and pieces—some bright and eye-catching (for drama and color), others subdued but sturdy. Held together by a unifying framework, it adds up to a useful and aesthetically pleasing whole.

Against this image of language as an ever-growing crazy quilt, the phenomenon of a shrinking vocabulary seems all the more tragic, almost inexplicable. Even as growing numbers of people receive a college education, their ability to understand words and use them correctly has been plummeting. To switch metaphors, it's as if we've inherited sacks of gold but live as paupers.

Fortunately the situation is reversible. The existence of this book—and the fact that you are reading it—indicates an awareness of the problem and a desire to do something about it. It's becoming obvious to many that the inability to use words effectively can have consequences ranging from detrimental (a missed sale) to fatal (confusing flight instructions). Conversely, knowing how to use words correctly and effectively can produce desirable results in everything from career advancement to civic involvement to personal relationships.

Note that word *effectively*. Loading your sentences with two-bit, sesquipedalian words is not effective communication. Your goal is to have an array of words to choose from and to use them wisely.

> *A good vocabulary enables us to communicate with greater subtlety and precision than a limited one. It's the difference between playing golf with a driver, nine-iron, and putter as against having a full set of clubs.*
> —Blake Clark

Behind my mélange of metaphors is one message: It takes a "full set of clubs" to unleash the power of words. How can you acquire a full set? Start with a dictionary and a thesaurus.

Searching for the Right Word

If you don't already own a good dictionary, buy one. Maybe more than one. Dictionaries each have their own strengths. Where one delves into word roots, others provide usage notes or more supplemental information.

If you're not sure which one to choose, look up a couple of words in one of the dictionaries offered by your local bookstore. "Heighth" and "irregardless" would do for your purposes. If the dictionary doesn't warn you that these are non-standard words (I call them non-words) and suggest replacing them with *height* and *regardless*, keep looking. If you don't find one that meets this criterion, try the used-book section.

Once you have a dictionary, use it! Wear it out! After a few years, buy another. That will keep you abreast of new words as they enter mainstream language and will alert you to shifts in meaning that may be under way.

Incidentally, I've never found the dictionary in my word processor to be much help. Besides, it's good exercise to get out of your chair and walk to wherever you keep your dictionary. It might even clear your head.

When you sit down to write and need a particular word, pause to consider the key ideas you want to convey. Start with a

word that's in the ballpark. Look it up and go from there, exploring synonyms, roots, and usage notes. Many's the time a usage note in the *American Heritage Dictionary* has led me to the word that fits, much as the right jigsaw puzzle piece slips into place.

> I compare it to the work of a stone cutter, chipping away at the raw material until it's just right, or as right as you can get it.
> —Harriet Doerr

If you're still stuck, try a thesaurus. From the Latin word meaning treasure, a thesaurus provides a treasure chest of possibilities—more than you can possibly dream up by yourself. A word of caution: The arrangement of words may be different from a dictionary. The alphabetical index in some thesauruses is in the back, and the front contains alternative wordings, grouped by function (e.g., eating, containers, foolishness). So when using this style of thesaurus, begin at the index in back.

Recently, I was looking for a colorful alternative to the word *group*. From the choices offered in the index, I selected *assemblage* as my starting point. This led me to words for groups of animals and birds: *flock, colony, drove, trip, pride* (lions), *sloth* (bears), *skulk* (foxes), *clowder* (cats), *gam* (whales), *skein* (geese in flight), *bevy* (quail), *watch* (nightingales), *charm* (finches), and *murmuration* (starlings). Eureka! What could be more colorful than a murmuration of language mavens! Of course, a cool head prevailed and I chose the more suitable *host*. But along the way, I was enriched by

my discovery of skulks and skeins, clowders and gams—
someday, I may have a use for them.

Your conscious hours are filled with words. What can you learn
from them? Observe the different ways people use words. Do
you find yourself guessing the meaning of some? Make a men-
tal note to look them up when you have the chance.

A great way to stretch your vocabulary is to read good books.
Notice each author's palette of words. Observe which work,
and which don't. Don't skip over unfamiliar words; you need
to make them your own. And be aware that some words coming your way need to be handled with caution.

Toxic English: A Self-Defense Manual for Consumers and Citizens

Not everyone who aims words at you has your enlightenment or entertainment in mind. Some people earn their living by talking you into buying something you don't need or can't afford. Hang on to your wallet!

Others who are skilled with words want to enlist your support for controversial, possibly shortsighted, policies.

> Language is the medium of politics, and as such it is subject to debasement by those in government who shape interpretations of their acts and policies for public consumption.—John Daniel

The techniques employed by politicians and advertisers can be both subtle and audacious. The following paragraphs suggest some things to watch for in order to detect obfuscation and chicanery. (Note: If you're not sure what obfuscation and chicanery are, now is a good time to exercise your linguistic muscles by looking them up.)

- The **passive voice** creates anonymity. Rivers are polluted, villages bombed, schoolyards contaminated. No one is responsible, these things just happen.

- **Avoidance words** cover up something more worrisome. The results of a lifetime of smoking hide under such phrases as *severe health effects* instead of cancer, emphysema, and heart disease. Vehicles are *preowned,* and public lands are *underutilized* (i.e., we're not letting enough cattle graze on them or minerals be extracted from them). War is hard to sell, so we have *armed intervention*, *no-fly zones*, and *police actions*.

- **The royal "we,"** the first-person plural (We think that . . .), suggests that we have all participated in decisions with far-reaching consequences. Like the passive voice, it diffuses responsibility, leaving no one truly accountable for what happens.

- **Exaggeration** results in an unending ramping up of adjectives, reaching for ever-greater intensity: *tremendous*, *unbelievable*, *revolutionary*, *spectacular*, *astronomical*. Eventually there's no place to go, and credibility is lost.

- **Distractors** make a task seem amazingly easy or risk-free: <u>Just</u> *sign here, a* <u>low</u> *12 percent interest rate,* <u>only</u> *$99.95.* Wiggle words like *virtually*, *nearly*, *as much as*, and *substantially* suggest more than is actually promised: *rust-resistant* (not *-proof*). Oxymorons slip by unnoticed: *99 percent cure*. Your attention is diverted by color, boldface, italics, capital letters, and exclamation points. Sympathy words such as *deserve* and *earn* play on self-pity: *You deserve a break—or a new sound system.*

- **Empty abstractions** such as *conceptualize* and *objective baseline indicators* leave you groping through the fog, unable to identify either excellence or incompetence.

Ken Smith, author of *Junk English*, calls this "the linguistic equivalent of junk food—ingest it long enough and your brain goes soft." But he adds that junk English is not inevitable. We made it; we can make it go away.

English on the Internet

Breaking the junk English habit may feel like an uphill battle when you're on the Internet. The sloppiness you see there suggests that many of us who use email or chat rooms forget there's a human being on the receiving end. We can't be bothered with being clear, concise, or polite. Perhaps the speed with which messages zip around the planet permeates the whole process, resulting in slapdash language and abbreviation to the point of incomprehensibility.

Remember, the person you're communicating with is probably just as hassled and sensitive as you are. Establish your own golden rule of the Internet, affirming that you will treat others as you want them to treat you. Choose your words carefully, check for typos and wrong or omitted words, aim for clarity—in short, be considerate. And don't use email for thank-you notes or messages of condolence; those call for a more personal approach.

. . .

From pictograms to the Internet: We've covered a lot in a few pages. But this survey of our linguistic legacy sets the stage for the words and phrases that follow. Among them you will find the right words to help you say what you really mean.

Standing on principal. See "principal, principle" on p. 120.

Tricky Words and Handy Phrases

Just what are Tricky Words? They are words that some people find confusing or troublesome.

- Words with small differences in spelling *(forego/forgo, home/hone)*.

- Words with different meanings and spellings but the same sound *(waist/waste; pour/pore; canvas/canvass)*.

- Words that are closely related and easily confused *(emigrate/immigrate; ecology/environment)*.

- Words that are misleading *(presently, inflammable)*; I call them **wrong-way words.**

- Words that are frequently mispronounced *(nuclear, realtor)* or misspelled *(memento)*.

- Words that aren't legitimate words *(complected, irregardless)*; I call them **non-words.**

- Words that are out-of-the-ordinary *(hubris, plethora)*.

Throw in some foreign expressions and a few words that just tickled my fancy, and that's what you'll find in the pages that follow.

How to Use This Section

To become acquainted with what's here, you might peruse the pages in the spirit of a Sunday drive. Dip in at random, then look up specific words that are a problem for you.

"What Do They Mean When They Say . . .?" and "Figures of Speech" answer some of your questions about how words are used. Altogether you'll find the unexpected and the useful, while developing a new appreciation of words.

An "as needed" philosophy prevails throughout the book. I've provided pronunciation guides and extended discussions of usage and derivations only where I considered them helpful.

When I do include a guide to pronunciation, accented syllables are capitalized, and long vowel sounds are indicated as follows:

a as in *able* = aa

e as in *easy* = ee

i as in *item* = ii

o as in *omen* = oh

u as in *union* = yew

According to this approximation of sounds, *Pronunciation Guide* is proh-NUN-see-AA-shun giid, and *United States* is yew-NII-ted STAATS.

I've used the following abbreviations:

adj., adjective

AHD, American Heritage Dictionary

Arab., Arabic

Fr., French

Ger., German

Gr., Greek

Heb., Hebrew

It., Italian

Lat., Latin

n., noun

OED, Oxford English Dictionary

Port., Portuguese

prep., preposition

Russ., Russian

Sans., Sanskrit

sing., singular

Sp., Spanish

Yid., Yiddish

v., verb

If you need to review the parts of speech, see the first volume of this trilogy, *Write Right! A Desktop Digest of Punctuation, Grammar, and Style*.

Starred entries are of special importance. By using those words correctly, you will be well on your way to having a solid foundation of "right words."

Tricky Words from A to Z

abbreviation, acronym, contraction, initialism: An abbreviation is a shortened version of a word or words (Mr., etc., U.S.). An acronym is the first letter or letters chosen selectively from a group of words in order to create a new word.

> light amplification by stimulated emission of radiation = laser
>
> What You See Is What You Get = WYSIWYG
>
> World Health Organization = WHO

A *contraction* is a shortened word in which some letters are replaced by an apostrophe *(can't, won't)*. An *initialism* is an acronym that is pronounced letter by letter rather than as a word *(NGO, AFL-CIO)*.

Unless the initialism or acronym is widely recognized *(RV, FBI, OPEC)*, use the full name the first time it appears, followed by the acronym in parentheses. You may then use only the acronym or initialism in subsequent references.

> United Nations Special Commission (UNSCOM)

abide, abide by: Used alone, the verb *abide* means to tolerate, endure, or stay with.

The campaign won't abide any racial slurs.

Their abiding faith in my skills touched me.

When the preposition *by* follows *abide*, the meaning of *abide* becomes comply with.

We will abide by your decision.

abrogate, arrogate, arrogant: *Abrogate* is a verb that refers to action terminating a treaty or agreement. *Arrogate* is a verb meaning to claim or take without right; *arrogant* is an adjective meaning haughty.

The FBI was accused of arrogating powers in their surveillance of terrorists.

When the U.S. abrogated the ABM Treaty, some considered it an arrogant move.

academic, moot: *Academic* means pertaining to a school *(his academic record)* or theoretical *(the discussion was an academic exercise)*. *Moot* in a legal context refers to the findings of an unofficial trial, which will neither be enforced nor serve as precedent. In common parlance, however, it has come to mean irrelevant *(a moot point)*.

a cappella (It., ah cuh-PEL-lah, "in the manner of the chapel [or choir]"): Singing that is not accompanied by musical instruments.

accede, exceed: To *accede* is to comply with or give in to; to *exceed* is to go beyond. There is no word spelled *excede*.

To accede to their demand exceeds the bounds of propriety.

We have reached a point in human history when the means of war have become so horrible that they exceed any possible good that can come from using them.—Howard Zinn

accept, except: The verb to *accept* is to receive or agree to.

She accepted an honorary degree.

I will accept those conditions.

The preposition *except* means excluding and should be followed by the objective case. See I, ME, MYSELF.

Everyone was on time except Celeste and me (*not* Celeste and I).

accused, alleged: Writers sometimes use these words in the belief that they provide protection from a lawsuit. They do not. Use *accused* only when formal charges have been filed against a suspect. *Alleged* indicates something that is said to be true, but isn't necessarily; in law, to *allege* suggests that proof will be forthcoming.

acoustics: When referring to the scientific study of sound, use a singular verb.

Acoustics <u>is</u> an area of special interest to me.
        sing.

When referring to the total effect of sound, use a plural verb.

The acoustics of the room <u>enhance</u> the performance.
                        plural

acronym. See ABBREVIATION.

acute, chronic: *Acute,* from a Latin word meaning sharp, applies to conditions that are sharp or intense and may reach a crisis rapidly. *Chronic*, from a word that refers to time, describes conditions that are lingering and recurring.

> The chronic shortage of funds at the homeless shelter produced acute distress among those denied help.

adept, proficient: Although the distinction between these two words is a fine one, *adept* indicates a natural aptitude that's improved by training; *proficient* suggests a high level of competence that has been achieved by training alone.

ad hoc (Lat., "toward this"): A committee formed to deal with one problem or set of problems. In informal use, *ad hoc* means slapdash, thrown together.

ad hominem (Lat., "to the man"): A personal attack rather than an attack on ideas or arguments; appealing to emotions and prejudices rather than to reason.

adieu, ado: The French word *adieu* (ah-DYEU), meaning good-bye, has made the trip into English; *ado* (uh-DOO) is a fuss or bother.

> Let's not make much ado about saying adieu.

ad infinitum (Lat., "to infinity"): Without end, limitless.

ad nauseum (Lat.): To a sickening or ridiculous degree.

adulation (n.): Extravagant praise.

adverse, averse (adj.): Generally, conditions are *adverse* (unfavorable, hostile), while people are *averse* (reluctant).

> In adverse market conditions, investors are often averse to buying high-risk stocks.

advice, advise: The noun *advice* means an opinion regarding how to proceed in a given circumstance. The verb *advise* means to give such an opinion, to inform.

> When the doctor advised you to stop smoking, he gave you good advice.

Advise often produces a stilted tone. Rewrite to avoid this.

> **Wrong:** Please advise whether you will be attending.

> **Right:** Please let us know if you will be attending.

aegis (n., EE-jis): Auspices, sponsorship.

> Care of dependent children remains under the aegis of the court.

affect, effect: Here's a rough guide to help you decide which word to use. If you're looking for a verb, chances are you want *affect,* which means to influence or to pretend in order to make an impression.

> The protestors hoped to affect the vote.

> The attorney affected a look of disbelief.

If you need a noun, *effect* is probably your word; it means outcome or result.

> The protest had the desired effect.

Less often used is the verb *effect,* which means to bring about, or to cause to occur.

> Through their actions, they hope to effect a change in policy.

The noun *affect* is limited to the field of psychology, where it refers to feeling or emotion, as distinguished from thought or action.

afflatus (Lat., uh-FLAA-tus): A sudden rush of divine or poetic inspiration. Bet that isn't what you thought it was!

aggravate, annoy, irritate: To *aggravate* is to make worse; to *annoy* is to bother; to *irritate* is to exasperate or provoke. As recently as the fourth edition of *Write Right!*, I wrote that conditions could be aggravated, but not people.

> My flu-like symptoms were aggravated by increased activity.

The juggernaut of usage seems to have rolled on, and some language authorities now accept *aggravate* in general usage to mean to be annoyed by.

> Loud noises late at night aggravate me.

Call me a nonconformist, but I still prefer *annoy* or *irritate* in such a sentence.

ain't: An odd contraction of *am not, are not, is not, have not,* or *has not,* in which letters are both added and omitted. Used in dialogue, casual speech, and when aiming for an effect.

> It just ain't so.

Though *ain't* has a long history, no doubt including use by Shakespeare, the taint of illiteracy persists. Avoid it in formal writing.

albeit (all-BEE-it): Since this borderline archaic word means *although*, it is redundant to precede it with the word *but*. Don't be afraid to use *albeit*—just use it correctly.

> Her apology was sincere, albeit somewhat tardy.

al dente (It., "to the tooth"): Cooked just enough to retain a somewhat firm texture.

alfresco (It.): Outdoors, in the open air. Also *al fresco*.

Eating al dente pasta al fresco.

algorithm: A mathematical term describing a computational procedure; you could call it a recipe for performing a calculation. (You get extra points for spelling it correctly.)

allege, contend: To *allege* is to formally state as a matter of fact what has not yet been proved. To *contend* is to dispute, to maintain or assert.

alleged. See ACCUSED.

allegory, fable, legend, myth, parable: An *allegory* is a story (e.g., *Pilgrim's Progress*) in which the principal characters represent qualities such as honesty or bravery, thus providing layers of meaning. A *fable* uses animals that speak in order to present a cautionary or edifying point (Aesop's *Fables*). A *legend* is an unverified popular story handed down from early times; a popularized myth of modern times; a person who achieves legendary fame *(a legend in his own time)*; and an explanatory caption for a map.

The *myths* that originated in preliterate society described the exploits of supernatural beings; they have become a way to express deep, commonly felt emotions and to embody cultural ideals. *Myth* now is also used broadly to refer to a misconception or notion based more on tradition or convenience than on fact. *(The invincibility of the Spanish Armada was a myth).* A *parable* is a simple story told to convey a moral or religious lesson.

alliaceous (ah-lee-AA-shus): Smelling or tasting of garlic or onion; an *alliaphage* is a garlic eater.

alliteration: Two or more words in sequence that begin with the same sound *(bouncing bubbles, nubile gnats gnawing on nuts).*

allude, elude: To *allude* is to refer indirectly; to *elude* is to slip away or to successfully avoid.

> I alluded to his shady past when I described how he was able to elude the law.

The noun form of the verb *allude* is *allusion*.

> His allusion to embarrassing moments on a first date made us laugh.

altar, alter: The noun *altar* is a platform or elevated structure at the front of a church or temple for use in religious ceremonies and celebrations. The verb to *alter* means to change or modify.

alternate, alternative: As a noun, *alternate* means a substitute *(she served as a jury alternate)*; as a verb, it means to occur in successive turns *(the mood alternated between hope and despair)*. As an adjective, *alternate* has been relaxed to mean every other *(the group meets on alternate Tuesdays)* and substitute *(take the alternate route)*.

Alternative indicates a choice, another possibility; it is no longer restricted to a choice between two options, but is acceptable when applied to two or more choices.

> We considered several alternatives to planting a formal garden.

ambiguous, ambivalent: *Ambiguous* means capable of having conflicting interpretations; *ambivalent* means having conflicting feelings, equivocal.

> His answer was purposely ambiguous.

> I'm ambivalent about going to the ball game.

ONE WORD OR TWO?

Careful writers use the one- and two-word forms of the words *almost, already, all right, altogether,* and *awhile* correctly; they have distinct meanings. To write "I am almost ready" indicates that you are nearly ready, but "You are almost welcome" suggests a cool reception rather than a warm one. Be sure to say what you mean.

Your remark was altogether inappropriate.

When all together, they often get the giggles.

Since *awhile* means for a short time, writing "for awhile" is redundant.

Wrong: I will stay for awhile.

Right: I will stay for a while, OR I will stay awhile.

See also WHILE.

Every day means each day; *everyday* means ordinary, routine. Other words with both one- and two-word forms include *into, setup, wakeup,* and words beginning with *any, every,* and *no (anyway, anyone, anybody, anytime, everyone, everybody, nobody).*

Note: Some one-word forms are not accepted as standard usage (e.g., *alot*). *Alright* is verging on acceptability, but for now, make it two words in formal writing: *all right.*

★ **amid, among, between:** Use *amid* with things that cannot be counted (*amid the turmoil*); use *among* with things that can be counted (*among likely voters*). Use *between* with two entities; otherwise, let your ear guide you.

> Between child care and job demands, young couples have little time to spare.

> Among certain tribes, potlatch is a well-established custom.

> Between innings, fans bought souvenirs.

Amidst has an archaic or British flavor, which isn't all bad. *Amongst*, though quaint to some ears, remains an acceptable variant of *among*.

amok (Malay, "murderous frenzy"): The expression "running amok" was originally applied to animals on a rampage, but it has been diluted over the centuries to describe a person who is out of control in some respect. The older spelling, *amuck*, is preferred in the United Kingdom.

> *Satire's my weapon, but I'm too discreet to run amuck.*
> —Alexander Pope

★ **amount, number:** Use *amount* with uncountable entities and *number* with countable ones.

> The number of voters who favor campaign finance reform is growing.

> They are concerned about the amount of influence that dollars buy.

amour propre (Fr., ah-MOOR PROH-preh): Self-respect.

amused, bemused: *Bemused* means puzzled, or deep in thought, not *amused*, which means entertained.

anachronism (uh-NAK-krun-izm): Anything out of its proper place in time.

> Listening to rappers makes me feel like an anachronism.

analogy, analogous: The noun *analogy* compares fundamentally dissimilar things that are alike in some respect.

> The speaker drew an analogy between a system of mass production and the boot camp approach to education.

The adjective form of the word is *analogous*.

> The speaker indicated that a system of mass production is analogous to the boot camp approach to education.

anathema: A person or thing that someone loathes; often followed by *to* and the name of the individual doing the loathing.

> Algebra is anathema to many students.

and/or: This is an inelegant shortcut. Rewrite to be more specific.

androgenous, androgynous: Both are adjectives pronounced an-DRAH-jen-us. *Androgenous* means pertaining to the production of male offspring; *androgynous* means having both female and male characteristics.

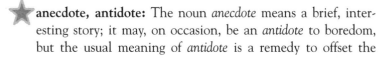**anecdote, antidote:** The noun *anecdote* means a brief, interesting story; it may, on occasion, be an *antidote* to boredom, but the usual meaning of *antidote* is a remedy to offset the

effects of a poison. "Anecdotal evidence" suggests a lack of proof.

The speaker began with an anecdote about his childhood.

The pharmacy stocks antidotes to a variety of poisons.

annihilate, decimate: To *annihilate* is to destroy completely. The literal meaning of *decimate* is to destroy one-tenth of something, but it is also loosely used to mean destroying a large part. To the careful writer, however, the words are not synonymous.

annoy. See AGGRAVATE.

annual, perennial: *Annual* means yearly; *perennial* means perpetual, recurring repeatedly. In botany, an *annual* is defined as a plant that completes its life cycle in a year or less; a *perennial* is a plant with a life span of two or more years.

antagonist, protagonist: An *antagonist* is one who opposes or competes with another; it is not an antonym of *protagonist*. *Protagonist* has strayed from its primary meaning of chief actor in a drama or other literary form; it now also means the central figure in an awkward or political situation.

ante, anti: Both are prefixes. *Ante-* means coming before; *anti-* means against.

The anteroom was decorated with antiwar posters.

To complicate things a bit, *anti* in the Italian word *antipasto* means before (specifically, before the first course).

ante-jentacular: Pre-breakfast; goes nicely with *post-prandial* (after dinner).

An **antigram** is a variation on the anagram, in which the newly created word or words are a wry comment on the starting word.

> astronomers = no more stars
>
> funeral = real fun

Not complicated enough? How about **anagrams** that give a clue to a pair of words, which are, in turn, anagrams of each other:

> drink fit for a king = regal lager
>
> hidden promise = latent talent
>
> object in outer space = remote meteor
>
> a drummer on the Concorde = supersonic percussion

anticipate: This verb means to look ahead and prepare for something, not simply to make a reasonable estimate.

> She anticipated my response.

anxious, eager: Reserve the word *anxious* for feelings of apprehension or foreboding. When looking forward with enthusiasm, or at least without anxiety, use *eager* or another word that corresponds with the feeling being described.

> She was anxious to learn the results of the bar exam.
>
> I'm eager to meet my new grandson (*or* can hardly wait, am looking forward to . . .)

anybody, anyone, anything, anyway, anywhere. See "One Word or Two?" on p. 29.

apophthegm (A-puh-them): An epigram. This makes two words with the letter sequence "phth" for you to wow your friends with. (The other is *ophthalmologist*). Also spelled *apothegm*, but that would be too easy. See EPIGRAM.

appraise, apprise: To *appraise* is to estimate the value of; to *apprise* is to inform.

> When the house has been appraised, please apprise us of the listing price you recommend.

appreciate: The verb *appreciate* means to increase in value or price; to be aware of.

> The value of their home had appreciated over the years.

> I appreciate your feelings in the matter.

However, some consider it a genteelism in a sentence like the following:

> I appreciate the trouble I've caused.

Rewrite, using such words as *realize* or *understand*. See GENTEELISM.

appropriate, expropriate: The adjective *appropriate* (uh-PROH-pree-ut) means suitable, proper. The verb *appropriate* (uh-PROH-pree-AAT) means to set apart for a specific use (*government-appropriated funds*); to take possession of, often without permission. To *expropriate* (ex-PROH-pree-AAT) is to exercise eminent domain over, to take by legal action private land for public use.

> My brother considered it entirely appropriate to appropriate my cookies.

The state expropriated my parents' land for a reservoir.

a priori (Lat., ah pree-or-ee, "from the previous"): Based on hypothesis or theory rather than on experiment or evidence; deductive.

The students used a priori reasoning to conclude that field trips are a valuable learning experience.

apropos (Fr., a-pruh-POH, "to the purpose"): The adjective *apropos* means fitting or pertinent *(an apropos assessment)*; as an adverb, *apropos* means with regard to *(apropos your remarks)*. Note that you don't say "apropos <u>of</u> your remarks."

apt, liable, likely, prone: Although these words are not synonyms for *probably*, they all indicate some degree of probability. *Apt* is appropriately used to indicate a tendency toward an activity or quality.

She is an apt student of languages.

Liable means legally obligated, responsible; it is the best choice when you want to imply possible risk or disadvantage.

You are liable for damages if you are at fault in a collision.

The adverb *likely* requires qualifiers such as *very* or *quite*.

We will quite likely be late.

The adjective *likely* does not need such qualifiers.

That's a likely story.

Likely and *apt* are interchangeable when followed by an infinitive *(likely to forget*, or *apt to forget)*. *Prone* suggests a tendency *(he is prone to exaggeration)* and also means lying face down. See PRONE.

arcane (adj.): Esoteric; known only to those having secret knowledge. It does not mean archaic.

arrant, errant: *Arrant* means unmitigated; *errant* means wandering, straying from the proper course.

> He saw himself as a knight-errant, while others perceived him as an arrant rascal.

arrogate, arrogant. See ABROGATE.

as, as if, like: Use *as* or *as if* to introduce a clause with a verb (i.e., when those words serve as conjunctions).

> She acted as if she had nothing on her mind.

> As I said, I won't be late.

Like is correct when it functions as a preposition and is followed by a noun or pronoun (*I wish I could stretch like my kitten*), and when it introduces a clause from which the verb has been omitted (*She reacted like a kitten to catnip*).

Bill Bryson points to the inconsistency of these rules by reminding us that *like* is used between the verb *feel* and an -ing verb, as in "I feel like singing." But we needn't always strive for a foolish consistency, which Emerson tells us is the hobgoblin of little minds.

as per: Strike this pair of words from your vocabulary. Rewrite.

> **Wrong:** As per your request, I enclose a widget.

> **Right:** I enclose the widget that you requested.

assert, claim: Careful writers distinguish between these verbs, though they are often used synonymously. *Claim* implies having evidence to back up an assertion, while to *assert* is to state one's position boldly. Some authorities declare that this battle is now over, and those who find *claim* to be stronger than *assert* or *contend* are free to use it. But the word may imply a lack of foundation, so use it with care.

> Isadora asserted that she was free to leave whenever she wanted.

> Rupert claimed that she hadn't changed the cat's litter box.

assure, ensure, insure: All three mean to make secure or certain, but each has a distinct flavor. *Assure* implies setting someone's mind at rest. *Ensure* and *insure* can be used interchangeably to mean securing from harm, but *insure* is the word to be used regarding policies for life or property.

ODDS & ENDS

Non-Words: Excise these from your vocabulary.

ahold	excape
alot	hinderance
alright	hunnert
anywheres	incidently
asterik	irregardless
boughten	nowheres
complected	publically
emote	simular

asterisk (ASS-ter-risk): The symbol * (which indicates a footnote) is sometimes mispronounced "asterik" or "asteriks."

attribute, credit: Use the verb *credit* when praise is deserved and the verb *attribute* (ah-TRIB-byewt) when simply assigning cause.

> The police attributed the fire to arson and credited a bystander with saving the life of an infant.

The noun *credit* has several meanings, including a source of honor or distinction (*She was a credit to the company*), a positive balance in one's bank account, and an amount that a bank or lending institution makes available to a client. The noun *attribute* (A-tri-byewt) means a characteristic or distinctive feature.

> They displayed all the attributes of inherited wealth.

auger, augur: The noun *auger* (AWE-grr) refers to a tool for boring into wood or earth; the verb *augur* (AWE-gyure) means to predict, usually from signs or omens.

auspicious (awe-SPIH-shus): An adjective describing promising circumstances, ones marked by success, not merely memorable (*an auspicious beginning*).

avant-garde (Fr., AH-vahnt GARD): This term is used both as a noun and as an adjective; it refers to the groundbreaking forefront of an artistic or intellectual movement and suggests being ahead of the times.

avenge, revenge: *Avenge* is a verb meaning to inflict punishment in response to an injustice, usually by someone other than the victim. *Revenge* is retaliation; it lacks the moral overtones of *avenge*.

average, mean, median: The adjective *average* means midrange, middling, sufficiency without distinction; it also means representative. In a statistical context, the nouns *average*, *mean*, and *median* have distinct meanings that should be observed in formal writing. *Average* is the number obtained by dividing a sum by the number of numbers that produced the sum. Thus, the average of 5, 10, and 15 is 10 (30 ÷ 3). A *batting average* is calculated by dividing the number of hits by the number of times at bat and then multiplying by 1,000.

The figure of 2.2 children per adult female was felt to be in some respects absurd, and a Royal Commission suggested that the middle classes be paid money to increase the average to a rounder and more convenient number.—Punch

The *mean* is the midpoint between the two extremes of a set of numbers, which often turns out to be the same as the *average*. Indeed, the most common type of average is referred to as the *arithmetic mean*.

The *median* is the middle number in a set of numbers; in other words, half of the numbers are higher than the median, and half are lower. This is straightforward for an odd-numbered set, say, 10, 20, 30, 40, and 50, where the middle number (and thus the median) is 30. In an even-numbered set, you have to average the two middle numbers in order to obtain the median. For the set consisting of 10, 20, 30, 40, 50, and 60, the two middle numbers are 30 and 40, and their average (the median) is 35.

averse. See ADVERSE.

avoid, evade: Both involve the concept of keeping away from, but *evading* employs devious means.

> He avoided confronting his former partner, who had been convicted of evading taxes.

awhile. See ALMOST and WHILE in "One Word or Two?" on p. 29.

axiom, corollary: An *axiom* is a proposition that is accepted as being self-evident or universally true; axioms are fundamental to deductive reasoning (i.e., reasoning that is inferred from general principles). A *corollary* is a proposition accepted as following with little or no effort from a proposition already established.

> An axiom of election reform is that money corrupts the political system.

> A corollary is the belief that eliminating large campaign contributions will have a beneficial effect on elections.

Vintage Ukuleles Sales, Lessons and
Entertainment for Hire

Onlyuke05@gmail.com
416 893 0802

Onlyuke.ca

Onlyuke.ca
Vintage Music Vintage Ukuleles

416 893 0802
Onlyuke05@gmail.com

Devoted to Vintage Ukuleles
Buy Sell Restore
Learn to Play

Bb

bad, badly: Errors associated with the word *badly* usually occur when it's used with the linking verb *feel*. The only correct way to use "I feel badly" is when describing a defective sense of touch. Otherwise, write "I feel bad."

When describing (or modifying) a verb, use an adverb (e.g., *badly, strongly*); when modifying a subject, use an adjective (*bad, strong*).

> I feel strongly that we should proceed. (*strongly* modifies the verb *feel*)

> The team feels bad about losing. (*bad* modifies the subject *team*)

bail, bale, baleful: The noun *bail* refers to the deposit required as an attempt to insure a defendant's appearance in court; the verb *bail* means to provide the required deposit.

> Her bail was set at $50,000. An anonymous donor bailed her out.

The verb *bail* also means to remove water from a boat.

The noun *bale* is a compact bundle (*bales of hay*); the verb *bale* means to put in a compact bundle (*We need to bale the hay*).

A *baleful* look is menacing, portending evil.

bait, bate: As a noun, *bait* is what you put on the end of a fish hook; as a verb, *bait* means to lure (especially with trickery) or to torment (especially with insult or ridicule). The verb *bate* means to moderate or reduce the force of; it is seldom used other than in the expression *bated breath*, though its cousin *abated* shows up in weather reports.

barbaric, barbarous: *Barbaric* is marked by crudeness (*barbaric manners*), *barbarous* by cruelty (*barbarous treatment*).

bare, bear: These two homophones suggest the wide variety of meanings that can be found in a couple of four-letter words. Which part of speech they are determines their meaning. *Bare*, as a verb, means to expose to view (*to bare his soul*); as an adjective, naked or minimum (*the bare facts*); as an adverb, just sufficient (*barely in time*). The many meanings of the verb *bear* include to support, have a tolerance for, give birth to, withstand, proceed in a given direction, and have relevance.

Sometimes the preposition that follows the verb determines the meaning; thus, *bear up* means to withstand, while *bear down* means to apply pressure. The noun *bear* refers to a big, furry animal. See BORN.

base, bass: *Base* is both a noun meaning headquarters, starting point, or ingredient, and a verb meaning to find a basis for, to establish. *Bass* has two pronunciations; the word with a long *a* sound is a homophone of *base* that means a low-pitched voice or musical instrument. When pronounced with a short *a* sound, *bass* refers to a variety of fish.

because of. See DUE TO.

bellwether: Someone or something that takes the lead or initiative; a trendsetter (*a bellwether stock*).

bemused. See AMUSED.

beside, besides: *Beside* is a preposition meaning next to or in comparison with. *Besides* is an adverb meaning moreover or in addition to.

> The bloody knife lay beside the crumpled body.

> She has many friends besides me.

bête noire (Fr., bet nwar): Literally black beast; pet peeve, bugbear.

better/best, worse/worst: To compare the merits of two things or people, use *better* or *worse*; for three or more, use *best* or *worst*.

between. See AMID.

between you and (I, me): Prepositions such as *between* call for a pronoun in the objective case; since *me* is an objective pronoun, it is the correct choice following a preposition. Would you say "Hold the tickets for I"? Obviously not. For the same reason, you shouldn't say "Hold the tickets for Emma and I." When confronted with a choice of pronoun, mentally remove the words that come between the preposition and pronoun to check which pronoun sounds right.

> to [you and] me

> for [him and] me

> from [her and] me

See also I, ME, MYSELF.

bi-, semi-: These Latin prefixes have distinct meanings. *Bi-* means two (*bicycle, bifocal*); *semi-* means half. Confusion arises in the context of time *(bimonthly, semimonthly)*. If you stick with the Latin meanings, you will avoid potential mix-ups.

> biweekly (-monthly, -annual) = every two weeks (months, years)

> semiweekly (-monthly, -annual) = twice each week (month, year)

billet-doux (Fr., bil-lay DOO, "sweet short note"): A love letter.

billion: In the United States, a billion has nine zeroes, in the United Kingdom, twelve. If there is any likelihood of confusion, specify which version you're using: two billion (U.S.) or two billion (U.K.).

bisect, intersect: To *bisect* is to cut at the midpoint; to divide into two equal portions. To *intersect* is simply to cut across or through, not necessarily at the midpoint.

blatant, flagrant: *Blatant* (adj.) suggests something that is obtrusive (such as noise or bluster) or offensively obvious *(blatant nonsense)*; *flagrant* implies willful, glaring wrongdoing.

> The official spouted blatant nonsense about reforms while continuing to commit flagrant violations of human rights.

bluestocking: Derisive term for an intellectual.

bona fide (Lat., BOH-nuh FIID, "in good faith"): Done or made in good faith; genuine, authentic. To present one's *bona fides* (BOH-nuh FII-dees) is to show credentials in order to prove qualifications or indicate achievement.

WORD ROOTS **Boondoggle** was coined in the 1920s by R. H. Link, an American scoutmaster, to describe the fussy braiding of a cord to be worn around the neck with a whistle or compass. Originally a label for a time-consuming hobby, it now designates government projects that waste taxpayers' money.

born, borne: Both are past participles of the verb to *bear*, but only *born* is used in the passive sense.

> He was born on the Fourth of July.

Otherwise, *borne* is the correct choice.

> She has borne 12 children.

> They have borne repeated insults.

Borne is also the correct choice in compound adjectives (*waterborne diseases, airborne particles*).

bourgeois (Fr., boor-zhwah): This noun originally referred to the free inhabitants of a *bourg* (town); it now generally refers to the property-owning class. The class made up of bourgeois is the *bourgeoisie* (boor-zhwah-zee).

breach, breech: *Breach* is a violation or infraction (*a breach of etiquette*); *breech* refers to part of a gun (*a breech-loading gun*), or the lower part of the human trunk (*breech delivery*).

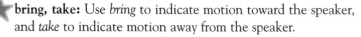**bring, take:** Use *bring* to indicate motion toward the speaker, and *take* to indicate motion away from the speaker.

> Take this application home and bring me the completed form tomorrow.

burglary, larceny, robbery, theft: *Burglary* is the crime of breaking and entering someone's home or place of business with the intention of committing a felony (e.g., theft). The standard verb form is *burglarize*, not *burgle*. *Larceny* and *theft* are synonyms for the act of taking someone's possessions. *Robbery* is theft from a person by force (actual or implied).

Cc

cabal (Fr., kah-BAL), **junta** (Sp., HOON-tah): A *cabal* is a conspiratorial group whose actions (which are also called a *cabal*) are directed against a government or political leader. A *junta* is a group of military officers who come to power after a coup.

callous, calloused, callus: The concept of hardening or thickening is at the root of these words. The noun *callus* describes a hardening of the skin.

I developed a callus where the shoe rubbed my toe.

The adjective *callous* means insensitive, hard-hearted (in other words, a hardening of the spirit).

Such callous behavior was indefensible.

But the adjective that means having calluses is spelled *calloused* (not callused). Go figure.

My calloused toe indicated that I needed new shoes.

If the verb form refers to a hardening of the spirit, use the *-ous* form; if it refers to physical thickening, use the *-us* form.

Such treatment calloused his attitude toward company loyalty.

The repetitive motion callused the children's fingers.

⭐ **can, may:** Reserve *can* for the possible, *may* for the permissible.

I may enter the race, but doubt that I can win.

canard (kan-NARD): A hoax or phony yarn.

cannon, canon: A large gun is a *cannon*; a list of officially approved works is a *canon*.

canvas, canvass: The noun *canvas* refers to a coarse, densely woven fabric; the verb *canvass* means to go through an area soliciting opinions, votes, sales, or the like.

⭐ **capital, capitol:** The term *capitol* is used only in connection with the buildings that house the U.S. Congress and the offices of state governments; the city in which a *capitol* building is located is the *capital*. The architectural term for the top part of a column is *capital*; wealth in the form of money or property is also referred to as *capital*.

Quite a lot of capital finds its way to the capitol.

Capital as an adjective means first rate (*a capital idea*); fatal (*a capital blunder*); requiring the death penalty (*capital punishment*); and an uppercase letter.

carat, caret, carrot, karat: The *-at* forms of these words (*carat, karat*) are variant spellings of the word that describes the weight of precious stones and metals. A *caret* (^) is a proofreading symbol indicating an insertion. We eat the other variety.

cardialgia: Heartburn; mild indigestion.

careen, career: *Careen* means causing to tilt from side to side; *career* means moving erratically at high speed. In popular usage, *careen* has essentially swamped *career*. "A loss for the language," opines Paul Lovinger, author of *The Penguin Dictionary of American English Usage and Style*. If you want to maintain the distinction, it may help to know that *careen* comes from the French word *carène*, the keel of a ship, which in turn may suggest leaning a ship on its side to clean and caulk the hull. *Career* comes from another French word, *carrière*, a racecourse, which suggests high speed.

> The huge waves made the ship careen between the dock and buoy.

> The soapbox racer careered down the hill before crashing into a tree.

The noun *career* refers to one's life work or chosen profession.

carpe diem (Lat., KAR-peh DEE-um): Seize the day. Go for it!

carte blanche (Fr., kart blahnsh, "blank card"): Unrestricted privileges; anything goes.

cause célèbre (Fr., kohz sel-LEB-bruh): Celebrated cause, sacred cow; something or someone given symbolic meaning.

cavort, consort: The verb *cavort* (ka-VORT) means to dance around, frolic, make merry. The verb *consort* (kun-SORT) is to associate with; the noun *consort* (KAHN-sort) is a companion or partner; a husband or wife, especially of a monarch.

> The queen's consort cavorted with their daughters.

The federal employee was suspected of consorting with a known agent.

celebrated, famous, infamous, notorious: *Celebrated* and *famous* mean being well known for commendable reasons. *Infamous* or *notorious* individuals, on the other hand, are known widely and regarded unfavorably; they are detestable.

celibate: To be *celibate* is to be unmarried; it does not mean merely refraining from sexual relations (the word for which is *chaste*).

Celsius, centigrade, Fahrenheit: All three are temperature scales. The freezing point of water is 0° on the Celsius and centigrade scales and 32° on the Fahrenheit scale. The boiling points are 100° and 212°, respectively. Celsius and centigrade are two names for the same scale, but Celsius has nudged out centigrade as the preferred term worldwide, especially in scientific usage. The United States has resisted converting to Celsius except in scientific circles, so our weather forecasts usually appear in degrees Fahrenheit. Since Celsius and Fahrenheit are named after individuals, their abbreviations are capitalized (°C, °F); no periods are used.

cement, concrete: A common error is to use *cement* in a sentence where *concrete* would be the correct word; they are not interchangeable.

Wrong: A cement sidewalk.

Right: A concrete sidewalk.

Concrete is composed of cement (a dry powder), aggregate (such as crushed rock), and water.

censor, censure: Despite their common root in a Latin word that means to judge or assess, these verbs have different meanings and pronunciations. To *censor* (SEN-ser) is to examine with the intention of prohibiting some form of expression; to *censure* (SEN-shur) is to sharply criticize or reprimand, especially in an open forum.

> Some parents want to censor what their children find on the Internet.

> The senator was censured for his behavior.

centrifugal, centripetal: These adjectives describe opposite forces. If you've ridden on the Tilt-a-Whirl at an amusement park, you have experienced both forces: the *centrifugal* (sen-TRIH-fyu-gul), which flings your head back, and the *centripetal*, which resists that pull.

chacun à son goût (Fr., shah-KUHN ah sohn GOO): Each to his own taste.

cherubim, seraphim: Both are orders of angels. *Seraphim* (the ones with wings) are the highest order; *cherubim* (the pink-cheeked, pudgy babies) are the second order.

childish, childlike: Both adjectives refer to behavior like that of a child, but *childish* is a pejorative term, indicating that behaving like a child is unsuitable in the circumstances (*a childish tantrum*), whereas *childlike* suggests an endearing quality (*childlike awe*).

chord, cord: A *chord* is a combination of musical notes, an emotional response, and a line segment that joins two points on a curve. A *cord* is a piece of rope or string, an electrical wire fitted with a plug, a unit of cut firewood, and an anatomical structure (*spinal cord* or *vocal cord*).

A chord can be produced by a quartet's vocal cords.

chronic. See ACUTE.

chutzpah (Yid., KHOOTZ-pah): Boldness, brazenness, impudent gall.

 Douglas Adams and John Lloyd, authors of *The Deeper Meaning of Liff*, define "liff" as a common object or experience for which no word yet exists. They seek to correct that situation in their book, which is chock-full of such useful words as Chimbote (CHIM-boh-taa), which they define as "a newly fashionable ethnic stew which, however much everyone raves about it, seems to you to have rather a lot of fish heads in it."

chimera (Lat., kii-MEER-uh): Castle in the air; unrealistic ambition. Originally referred to an imaginary monster or unjustified fear.

circa (Lat., SIR-kuh): Abbreviated ca. A term meaning around or approximately, which is used when indicating an approximate date (*ca. 1939*).

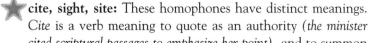**cite, sight, site:** These homophones have distinct meanings. *Cite* is a verb meaning to quote as an authority (*the minister cited scriptural passages to emphasize her point*), and to summon before a court of law (*the officer cited me for speeding*). *Sight* is a

noun meaning vision and a verb meaning to see *(the sailor sighted land)*. The noun *site* is a location *(building site)*, and the verb *site* means to locate *(the building was sited on a steep slope)*.

claim. See ASSERT.

cleave (v.): Columnist Theodore Bernstein calls this a two-faced word; it means both to split apart and to cling to. Either use has an archaic flavor.

> Your words cleaved my heart.

> The diaphanous gown cleaved to her body.

climactic, climatic: *Climactic* refers to a climax, while *climatic* refers to the weather.

cognoscenti (It., kohn-nyoh-SHEN-tee): The most informed members of a group.

cohort: *Cohort* is a Middle English word derived from the French *cohorte* meaning enclosed yard, company of soldiers, or multitude. It is appropriately used when referring to a group of people joined in a common endeavor or having a common characteristic (e.g., age, level of education). Although the prefix *co-* suggests a single individual (as in *coauthor* or *codependent*), there is no "hort" to be "co" with. Do not use it to refer to an individual; instead use words such as *colleague*, *friend*, or *accomplice*.

> The psychologist tested a cohort of first-year college students.

collegial, collegiate (adj.): Use *collegial* in a friendly reference to a colleague, and *collegiate* with reference to a college.

The university encourages a collegial atmosphere at all collegiate events.

Colombia, Columbia: *Colombia* is a South American country; the District of *Columbia* is the capital of the United States.

common, mutual, reciprocal: *Common* applies to something shared by two or more individuals or things without implying any further relationship (*a common interest*). *Mutual* suggests something shared (*mutual respect*), while *reciprocal* suggests something exchanged (*a reciprocal agreement*).

compare to, compare with: When likening one thing to another, use *compare to*.

> *Shall I compare thee to a summer's day?*—Shakespeare

When examining two or more things to discover the similarities and differences, use *compare with*.

> Some studies comparing test scores with intelligence have been shown to be flawed.

Theodore Bernstein finds that the "to" uses are usually more abstract or figurative, the "with" uses more literal.

compel, impel: The distinction between these two verbs may be a fine one, but it is useful. *Compel* suggests being forced to act in a certain way, while *impel* indicates some willingness on the part of the person acting.

> The windfall impelled me to go on a shopping spree.

> My overdrawn account compelled me to cut expenses.

complected: A non-word; use *complexion*.

> A dark complexion (*not* dark complected)

complement, compliment: Use *complement* (with an *e*) when it means to complete or enhance something; use *compliment* (with an *i*) to praise or express admiration.

> The smooth vanilla flavor complements the spiciness of the ginger. My compliments to the chef!

The word to use when describing something free is *complimentary (complimentary tickets)*.

complete, replete: Something that is *complete* has all the necessary parts. However, be careful when using qualifiers with *complete*.

> **Wrong:** This report is very complete.

> **Right:** J's report is more complete than K's.

Replete means plentifully supplied and is usually accompanied by the word *with*.

> The letter, replete with expletives, was submitted as a prank.

compound, confound: One of the meanings of the verb *compound* is to worsen, to add to; to *confound* is to create confusion, to puzzle.

> Bad weather compounded the problems facing the rescue team.

> The ending of the play confounded the critics.

Some authorities resist the use of *compound* to mean worsen since the word already has many other meanings (to combine, to compute interest on principal). Alternatives to *compound* may be a better choice (e.g., intensify, exacerbate, add to).

> Bad weather added to the problems of the rescue team.

comprise: *Comprise* means to contain, to consist of. Thus, to write "comprised of" is to double up on *of*.

> The company comprises (*or consists of*) four divisions.

> Four divisions constitute the entire company.

Language authority Sir Ernest Gower describes the lamentably common use of *comprise* as a synonym for *compose* or *constitute* as "a wanton and indefensible weakening of our vocabulary." Lest you be accused of furthering such wanton weakening, use *is composed of* or *consists of* rather than *comprised of*.

compulsion, compunction: *Compulsion* is an irresistible urge to do something, though it may be irrational. *Compunction* is a strong uneasiness produced by a feeling of guilt.

> Do you have any compunctions about your compulsion to raid the refrigerator late at night?

condone: No sense of approval should be implied when you use *condone*. It means to overlook or forgive.

confidant/confidante, confident: A *confidant* (KAHN-fee-DAHNT) is a close friend (male or female), someone you might confide in; the feminine spelling, *confidante*, is not generally used in the United States. To be *confident* (KAHN-fih-dent) is to be self-assured or certain of success.

> Tamara, my childhood confidant, is confident she will win the election.

connive, conspire: *Connive* comes from the Latin word that means to close one's eyes. Thus, someone who winks at an uncomfortable truth is *conniving*. *Conspire* comes from the Latin word meaning to breathe together; individuals who work toward a common end are *conspiring*.

> Circumstances conspired to prevent my attending.

The noun *conspiracy* adds the element of secrecy.

connote, denote: To *denote* is to point out, to show or indicate; to *connote* (the more commonly used word) is to suggest or imply. The term "apple pie" *denotes* an edible item consisting primarily of a crust and apple filling. The same pie might *connote*, among many possibilities, the aroma and taste of cinnamon and apples, close family feelings—that motherhood stuff.

consensus: Two common errors occur with this word. It is frequently misspelled (there is no "census" in *consensus*), and it often appears with the unnecessary "of opinion." *Consensus* means collective opinion, so *consensus of opinion* is redundant.

contagion, infection: *Contagion* is the transmission of disease by direct or indirect contact with a carrier of the disease. A *contagious* disease is catching; it tends to spread from one person to another. But an *infection*, which results from an invasion of a part of the body by pathogenic organisms, is not contagious. A cut that becomes infected is an example. Despite this difference, both *infectious* and *contagious* are used figuratively to indicate something catching (*an infectious laugh*, *a contagious yawn*).

contemporaneous, contemporary: Both adjectives mean occurring or existing at the same time. *Contemporaneous* is used with respect to events, *contemporary* with respect to people. *Contemporary* also has the meaning of modern or present-day.

> While I was attending a lecture on contemporary architecture with a contemporary of mine, I missed the contemporaneous steel-drum performance.

contemptible, contemptuous: Something that is *contemptible* is worthy of contempt; someone who is *contemptuous* shows contempt.

continual, continuous: *Continual* means repeatedly, occurring again and again; *continuous* is unending, without interruption.

> Your continual interruptions are annoying.

> The film is being shown continuously.

Theodore Bernstein provides a mnemonic for word freaks:

> continu<u>ous</u> = <u>o</u>ne <u>u</u>ninterrupted <u>s</u>equence

Well, maybe you should just consider using either *incessant* or *intermittent*.

contretemps (Fr., KON-tre-TAHn): A misadventure or embarrassing situation.

⭐ **convince, persuade:** To *convince* means getting someone to believe something; to *persuade* means getting someone to do something.

> The jurors were convinced of the defendant's innocence.

> The chairman persuaded me to act as recording secretary.

Convince is usually followed by *of* or *that*, *persuade* by *to*.

> *If you are convinced of the difference between these two words, perhaps you will be persuaded never to use an infinitive after convince.*—Theodore Bernstein

⭐ **cope:** Though popular usage has people coping (i.e., managing), a careful writer will restrict its use to coping *with* something.

> Parents of twins learn to cope with little sleep.

corpus delicti (Lat., KOR-pus dee-LIK-tii, "the body of the crime"): The physical evidence that a crime has been committed.

could of: To make this into good English, use *could have*.

> I could have won the contest if I had entered on time.

⭐ **council, counsel, consul:** A *council* is a committee or group of people; *counsel* is a verb meaning to advise or a noun meaning someone who gives advice; *consul* is an individual appointed by a government to represent business interests in a foreign country.

> Although the city's counsel advised council members of possible lawsuits, they chose to ignore her counsel.

> Some countries have consuls in major cities throughout the world.

coup de grâce (Fr., KOO deh GRAHS, "stroke of mercy"): A death blow; any finishing or decisive stroke.

coup d'état (Fr., KOO daa-TAH, "stroke of state"): An overthrow of the government; shortened to *coup*. In popular usage, *coup* also means a personal triumph.

credible, creditable, credulous: All three are adjectives. *Credible* means believable (the noun form of this word is *credibility*); *creditable* is reputable or worthy of esteem. *Credulous* means believing too readily and is more commonly used in its negative form, *incredulous*.

> That I could play a creditable game of poker is barely credible, so my friends were incredulous when I told them I had won.

criteria, criterion: A standard or rule for basing a decision is called a *criterion*; if more than one rule or standard is involved, use the plural form, *criteria*. Use a singular verb with *criterion* (*criterion is*) and a plural verb with *criteria* (*criteria are*).

> **Wrong:** A wise choice usually involves more than one criteria.

> **Right:** A wise choice usually involves more than one criterion.

See *Write Right!* for a table of singular and plural forms of such Latin words as *criterion* and *phenomenon*.

Dd

damp, dampen: To *damp* the oscillation of a wave is to reduce its amplitude.

> Deep sand would strongly damp the oscillation of a rocking chair.

To *dampen* is to moisten; it's what you do to clothes before you iron them.

> **Wrong:** The material has improved sound-dampening qualities.

> **Right:** The material has improved sound-damping qualities.

data: *Data* is the plural form of the Latin word *datum*, meaning information (especially numerical information). Other than in scientific writing, *data* is usually treated as a singular word. Nonetheless, some writers consider it elegant and precise to use *data* as a plural. So if you're striving for elegance and precision, use a plural verb with *data*; if it's the common touch you're after, use a singular verb. Kingsley Amis has yet another approach: Simply avoid the word, while enjoying a comfortable little thrill of superiority whenever you spot a singular use.

decimate. See ANNIHILATE.

déjà vu (Fr., "already seen"): An overworked expression that describes the illusion of having experienced something before.

de jure (Lat., deh zhyoor), **du jour** (Fr., doo zhyoor): The Latin *de jure* means according to the law.

> The defendants were found innocent de jure, though many considered them to be guilty nonetheless.

The French *du jour* means of the day *(soup du jour)*.

delegate, relegate: To *delegate* is to assign a task or responsibility without the negative connotation that *relegate* carries. To *relegate* is to assign to a lower position; to banish.

delusion, illusion: A *delusion* is the conviction that something that is untrue is true *(delusions of grandeur)*; the verb form is *delude*.

> I deluded myself into thinking that I could learn to speak Japanese quickly.

An *illusion* is a false impression; an erroneous perception of reality *(an optical illusion)*.

> *That the sun moves round the earth was once a delusion, and is still an illusion.*—H. W. Fowler

demise: This noun refers to the death of something, not to its decline.

denote. See CONNOTE.

dénouement (Fr., DAY-noo-MAHn, "an untying"): Undoing of a knot; final unraveling or completion of a plot.

de novo (Lat., deh NOH-voh): Anew; afresh.

deprecate, depreciate: To *deprecate* (DEH-pre-kaat) is to put down or belittle; to *depreciate* (deh-PREE-shee-aat) is to diminish in price, to lose value.

> He resented the way his opponent deprecated his record of service.

> As soon as you buy a new car, its resale value starts to depreciate.

de rigueur (Fr., deh ree-GRR, "of rigor"): Required by custom or fashion; socially obligatory.

desert, dessert: The noun *desert* (DEZ-urt) is a hot, dry place; the verb *desert* (deh-ZURT) means to abandon. Use *dessert* (deh-ZURT), the word with the extra *s*, when you mean the sweet extra course we put at the end of a meal.

> In the desert, we were served ice cream for dessert. When the temperature soared, we deserted the place.

When coupled with the word *just*, the noun *desert* means something deserved (usually a punishment); this plural usage is pronounced deh-ZURTS.

> As the one who had suggested bungee jumping, I got my just deserts when I was chosen to be first.

desideratum (Lat., day-sid-err-RAH-tum): Something needed and desired.

détente (Fr., day-TAHNT): Easing of strained relations.

deter: Since *deter* means to discourage or prevent an action, it should refer to people, not things.

> The graphic images deterred the students from drinking and then driving (*not* deterred drinking and driving).

detract, distract: To *detract* is to take away from, to diminish; to *distract* is to divert attention. Thus, someone who is distracted is not paying attention, and loud talking would detract from my enjoyment of a concert.

deus ex machina (Lat., DAY-us eks MAH-kee-nah, "God from the machine"): A plot device to tie up all the loose ends.

Doublets: A game invented by Lewis Carroll, Doublets starts with two words of the same length (e.g., *pig* and *sty, head* and *tail*). The object is to work your way from the first word to the last in as few steps as possible, while changing just one letter per step.

PIG-wig-wag-way-say-STY (four links)

HEAD-heal-teal-tell-tall-TAIL (four links)

MORE-lore-lose-loss-LESS (three links)

---

dharma (Sans., "law"): That which binds and sustains; in Buddhism, the law of Buddha.

differ from/with: To *differ from* is to be unlike; to *differ with* is to disagree.

different from/than: For simple comparisons, use *different from*.

> Their approach is different from mine.

When a clause follows, *different than* is acceptable usage. Either *from* or *than* would work in the following sentence.

> My approach, which is different than (from) what my mother taught me, is to try anything once.

different, varied, various: *Different* means unlike. *Varied* means having various forms or kinds; modified or altered. *Various* means several, of diverse kinds, one of a class or group. Avoid the redundant expression "various different."

The outcome was different from what we had expected.

The details varied but the outcome remained the same.

Various factions tried to affect the outcome.

diffident, indifferent: *Diffident* is an adjective meaning timid, lacking self-assurance; the adjective *indifferent* describes someone who is aloof or fails to show an interest when it would be appropriate to do so.

The diffident manner in which he approached the microphone suggested that he was not used to public speaking.

Having made up her mind, she was indifferent to the child's pleas.

dilemma, predicament, Hobson's choice: Reserve *dilemma* for a choice between two unpalatable alternatives; use *predicament* for a generally troublesome situation.

The dilemma voters face when choosing between two undesirable candidates constitutes a national predicament.

Often incorrectly used to indicate a difficult choice, *Hobson's choice* means an apparently free choice when there is no real alternative. It is named for a 17th-century liveryman who required his customers to take the next available horse.

disassemble, dissemble: The noun *disassemble* means to take apart; the verb *dissemble* means to present a false appearance, to disguise.

Disassembling the appliance was a frustrating job, but she dissembled by telling jokes.

disburse, disperse: The concept of distribution is common to both of these words, but *disburse* means to pay out from a fund, while *disperse* means to scatter in many directions, as police disperse a crowd.

discreet, discrete: People who are *discreet* exercise proper caution or judgment. Particles that are *discrete* are separate.

A few discreet inquiries revealed their discrete locations.

disingenuous, ingenious, ingenuous, insincere: To be *disingenuous* is to be crafty, not straightforward; to be *ingenious* is to be clever, inventive; to be *ingenuous* is to be naïve, innocent; to be *insincere* is to be hypocritical, to feign beliefs or feelings not held.

disinterested, uninterested: To be *disinterested* is to be impartial; to be *uninterested* is to lack interest.

dispute, rebut, refute, repudiate: To *dispute* is to question the validity of something. To *rebut* is to present contrary evidence. To *refute* is to show conclusively that an allegation is wrong. To *repudiate* is to deny the validity of something.

distinctive, distinguished: *Distinctive* is unmistakable, set apart; *distinguished* suggests eminence.

A distinctive odor emanated from the distinguished professor's corpse.

diverge: Reserve this verb for situations in which things are moving apart, not merely differing.

Their routes diverged after they left Cairo.

donnybrook: A brawl or uproar.

doppelgänger (Ger., DAHP-ul-GANG-er, "double goer"): A double or twin, especially one who is pernicious, ghostly, or haunting.

due to, because of: According to a now widely ignored rule, you should use *due to* following forms of the verb *to be* and *because of* in cause-and-effect situations.

> His bad posture was due to years of sitting hunched over a keyboard.

> He didn't qualify for the Army because of his bad posture.

There's not a lot of grammatical justification behind this rule, so use whichever sounds better.

Ee

each: *Each* is a singular pronoun; thus, when it is the subject, it requires a singular verb.

> Each of the students is welcome to attend.

However, when *each* follows a plural subject, the verb is unaffected by *each* and remains plural.

> The students each have their own lockers.

eager. See ANXIOUS.

ecology: A study of the relationship of organisms to their environment; not a synonym for environment or surroundings. See also ENVIRONMENT.

effect. See AFFECT.

effective, effectual, efficacious, efficient: To be *effective* is to be competent; to be *effectual* is to achieve the desired result. *Efficacious* is a rather pompous synonym for *efficient*, which means to get things done economically and in a timely manner. The opposite of these conditions is indicated by adding the prefix *in-* (*inefficient*, etc.).

e.g., i.e.: These abbreviations of Latin words are not interchangeable. Use *e.g.* (*exempli gratia*, meaning "for example") when you are providing one or more examples. Use *i.e.* (*id est*, meaning "that is") when you are elaborating on a point. Be sure to put a comma following the abbreviation.

> The cooking contest included some unusual entries (e.g., chess pie, flannel hash, and hush puppies).

> I had to resolve the dilemma (i.e., choosing between a moonlight flotilla and skinny-dipping).

élan (Fr., aa-LAHn): Enthusiasm, flair.

elegy, eulogy: You might read an *elegy* (a mournful poem) as part of a *eulogy* (a speech honoring someone who died recently).

eliminate, obviate: To *eliminate* is to get rid of, to remove. To *obviate* is to make unnecessary.

> By eliminating the contest, we obviated the need to find judges.

elude. See ALLUDE.

emanate, eminent, immanent, imminent: *Emanate* is a verb meaning to shine or issue forth from; *eminent* is an adjective meaning well-known or distinguished; *immanent* is an adjective meaning inherent, existing or remaining within; *imminent* is an adjective meaning about to happen.

> The eminent psychic emanated an unearthly glow as he hinted that the end was imminent.

> Some see God as immanent in nature.

emigrate, immigrate: Both of these verbs refer to motion to or away from a country. You emigrate when you leave or exit from a country; you immigrate when you come into a country.

employ, use, utilize: To *employ* is to put into service (in addition to its meaning of hiring someone). *Use* is the most general of these terms, meaning to employ for some purpose. *Utilize*, when not simply an attempt to sound impressive by using multisyllabic words, indicates finding new uses for something or someone.

> The instructor employed a variety of techniques in teaching the class how to use the Internet.

> She hopes to find a job that will utilize her linguistic talents.

energize, enervate: To *energize* is to rouse or give energy to; its antonym, *enervate*, means to sap the strength of, to weaken.

enfant terrible (Fr., ahn-fahn ter-REE-bleh): Terrible child; a talented youngster who breaks the rules.

ennui (Fr., AHn-WEE): Boredom.

enormity, enormousness: Since *enormousness* is an awkward word that sounds rather made up, people sometimes choose *enormity* to describe large size. But *enormity* implies immoral or outrageous behavior and should be reserved for such usage (*the enormity of the crime*). To convey large size, choose such alternatives to *enormousness* as *immensity*, *vastness*, or *hugeness*.

ensure. See ASSURE.

enthuse: "Back formations" such as *enthuse* (formed from the word *enthusiasm*) sometimes become acceptable to usage experts. *Enthuse* isn't there yet. Write "is enthusiastic about."

entomology, etymology: *Entomology* is the branch of science that studies insects; *etymology* is the branch of linguistics that studies origins of words.

environment: This word means surroundings. Avoid vague references to "the environment" when you mean nature or the world. Instead, use more precise words.

> **Vague:** Acid rain is harmful to the environment.

> **Specific:** Acid rain has killed fish and aquatic plants in nearby rivers and lakes.

Environment can also refer to non-physical surroundings (*an environment of fear*).

epicure. See GOURMAND.

epigram, epigraph: An *epigram* is a short, often witty, saying. An inscription on a public building or a quotation appearing at the head of a chapter is an *epigraph*. The final syllable of *epigraph* (which comes from a Greek word meaning "written") may help you remember that it's the written one.

epitaph, epithet: *Epitaph* can be either an inscription on a tombstone or a brief tribute to a dead person. An *epithet* is a term used to characterize an individual or entity (ambulance chaser, angel of mercy, the Beltway). An epithet need not be derogatory, though it is increasingly interpreted that way. *Epithets* are often hurled, which is not something you do with a compliment.

equable, equitable: *Equable* means unvarying, even-tempered; *equitable* means fair.

> Her equable demeanor contributed to an equitable solution.

equivalent, equivocal: *Equivalent* means equal to or the same as; *equivocal* is ambiguous, open to more than one interpretation.

> Her equivocal response to his proposal was equivalent to a "No."

errant. See ARRANT.

erratum (Lat.): Error; the plural is *errata*.

error, fallacy: An *error* is a mistake. A *fallacy* is a false notion, a statement that may mislead by being illogical or erroneous.

The idiosyncrasies of English have provided Richard Lederer with the material for a career of lectures and books. Here are a few of the absurdities he points out:

Boxing rings are square.

A slim chance and a fat chance are the same, but a wise man and a wise guy are opposites.

Quite a few and quite a lot are alike, but overlook and oversee are opposites.

You fill in a form by filling it out.

Sweetmeats are candies, while sweetbreads, which aren't sweet, are meat.

esprit de corps (Fr., ess-PREE de KOR): The spirit of enthusiasm and devotion of a group.

etc.: An overworked abbreviation of the Latin *et cetera,* meaning "and the others." Use it sparingly to indicate some other, unnamed items of a similar nature. Never write or say the redundant "and etc."

eulogy. See ELEGY.

euphemism: A *euphemism* is the substitution of less offensive words for those considered offensive. Thus, drunkenness might be referred to as "a condition of nonsobriety." Obviously, what one finds offensive is an individual matter. For some, describing bodily functions or other personal information calls for the roundabout nature of euphemisms ("I need to see a man about a dog," "in the family way"); others find it offensive when the irradiation of food is called "cold pasteurization."

euro: The unit of currency of the European Union; it is not capitalized.

evade. See AVOID.

⭐ **evoke, invoke:** To *evoke* is to elicit, to summon or bring forth; to reawaken; to produce a reaction. To *invoke* is to cite in support of one's cause; to call upon for assistance, especially a higher power.

> Her words evoked memories of lazy summer afternoons.

> The mayor invoked an obscure ordinance to deny the permit.

⭐ **exacerbate, exasperate:** To *exacerbate* (egs-AS-ser-baat) is to aggravate or increase the severity of a problem, pain, or emotion; it does not mean simply to increase. An antonym of *exacerbate* is *ameliorate*. To *exasperate* (egs-ASS-per-aat) is to provoke or tax the patience of someone.

> The ease of obtaining cigarettes exasperates parents because it exacerbates the problem of smoking among young people.

exalt, exult: To *exalt* is to raise in position or character, to glorify; to *exult* is to celebrate joyfully, to be jubilant or triumphant.

exceed. See ACCEDE.

except. See ACCEPT.

ex officio (Lat.): By virtue of office or position; describes the role of someone serving on a committee in an informal or advisory capacity.

ex parte (Lat., eks PAR-tee): From one side; partisan.

expedient, expeditious: *Expedient* means serving the purpose at hand; a politic, but not necessarily principled, action. An action that is undertaken quickly and efficiently is *expeditious*.

> The increase in bus fare was viewed as an expedient that was needed in order to meet the deficit expeditiously.

explicit, implicit: Something that is clearly and directly stated is *explicit*; if it is implied or understood but not stated, it is *implicit*.

ex post facto (Lat.): After the fact; a retroactive action that refers to something that came before. See also IPSO FACTO.

extemporaneous. See IMPROMPTU.

Ff

fable. See ALLEGORY.

Fahrenheit. See CELSIUS.

fait accompli (Fr., FAY tah-cohm-PLEE): A completed action.

fallacious, plausible, specious: Something that is *fallacious* is founded on mistaken logic or perception, wrong on the face of it. *Plausible* means apparently valid, likely, or acceptable; it also means giving a deceptive aura of truth, seemingly valid.

Specious is seemingly sound or true, but actually not. In other words, the distinctions between these adjectives are not sharp.

fallacy. See ERROR.

famous. See CELEBRATED.

farther, further: In 1977, Theodore Bernstein forecast that 50 years hence, people would not have to worry about the distinction between these two words, because "*farther* is going to be mowed down by the scythe of Old Further Time." We haven't yet arrived at 50 years, so let's continue to use *farther* where physical distance is involved (*I ran farther today than yesterday*), and *further* to indicate to a greater degree (*I'm looking into the matter further*).

fatwa: An Islamic declaration of a death sentence.

faux pas (Fr., foh pah): False step; mistake, social blunder.

faze, phase: *Faze* is not an informal spelling of *phase* but a legitimate verb meaning to disturb or disconcert. *Phase* as a verb means to carry out something in stages; as a noun, it is a period of development or cycle of events.

> My teenage phase didn't faze my parents.

feasible, possible, practicable, practical, workable: All these adjectives express varying degrees of suitability for use or being put into effect. *Practical* suggests assured success, acquired through practice or action. Results may be uncertain when something is *practicable*; you may be able to do something, but might not want to. *Possible* indicates something that may (or may not) occur. *Feasible* suggests something clearly possible and applicable. *Workable* forecasts a high likelihood of success.

fewer, less: Use *fewer* with things that can be counted, *less* with quantities considered as a whole, or as a single item: fewer jobs, less income.

> The tickets cost less than $50. ($50 is considered as a unit, not as individual bills.)

> Fewer than 500 people attended.

This express line has a grammatically correct sign.

Word Squares consist of the arrangement of words in squares so as to create legitimate words in more than one direction.

Single-word squares (same word in two directions):

```
L A N E          C R E S T
A R E A          R E A C H
N E A R          E A G E R
E A R S          S C E N E
                 T H R E E
```

Doubleword squares (horizontal and vertical words differ):

```
O R A L
M A R E
E V E N
N E A T
```

 figuratively, literally: *Figurative* serves as an advisory, suggesting that the reader not interpret imaginative language as reality.

> I was speaking figuratively when I said I would jump off a cliff.

Many writers and speakers create graphic images without using the word *figurative*.

Analisa made a killing in real estate.

Jeremy buried the opposition.

A common error is to use *literally* for emphasis; indeed, some dictionaries define *literally* as actually or really. But careful writers will observe what the word itself suggests: letter for letter (or word for word) accuracy.

Wrong: I literally exploded when I heard the news.

Right: The group sought the literal destruction of the tenement.

figure: As a verb, *figure* is considered to be informal usage.

Did you figure out the ending ahead of time?

Go *figure* and *it figures* are decidedly informal.

fix: Though *fix* is used in casual conversation, you should replace it in careful writing with more specific verbs, such as *repair*, *locate*, or *prepare*.

flack, flak: *Flack* is a variant spelling of *flak*, which means anti-aircraft fire (an acronym from the German <u>Fl</u>iegerab<u>w</u>ehr<u>k</u>anonen). *Flack* is also a slang expression for excessive criticism or for a person who works in public relations.

flagrant. See BLATANT.

flagrante delicto (Lat., flah-GRAHN-taa deh-LIK-toh): Caught in the act. The complete expression is *in flagrante delicto*.

flammable, inflammable: Both words mean capable of burning. To avoid confusion, use *flammable*.

flaunt, flout: To *flaunt* is to show off or proudly display; to *flout* is to defy or ignore.

> They flouted the authorities by flaunting their low-cut gowns.

flounder, founder: When you *flounder*, you move clumsily as you attempt to regain your balance. When you *founder*, you collapse. When a horse *founders*, it goes lame; when a ship *founders*, it sinks.

forbid, prevent, prohibit: All these words are concerned with keeping something from happening. To *forbid* is to command not to do something. To *prevent* is to successfully impede, to hinder; it is often followed by a gerund, which should be preceded by a possessive pronoun.

> My illness prevented my being there (*not* prevented me being there).

To *prohibit* is to forbid by authority. *Prohibit* is used with the preposition *from*; *forbid* is used with the preposition *to*.

The sign prohibited individuals from trespassing.

I forbid you to go.

forceful, forcible: *Forceful* means persuasive or effective (*a forceful speaker*). *Forcible* refers to something accomplished by force (*forcible entry*).

force majeure (Fr., fors mah-JOOR): Superior or magnificent force, such as a hurricane, which prevents meeting a deadline or fulfilling a contract.

The contract included a force majeure clause.

forego, forgo: The distinction between these two verbs is often *forgone*, but if you want to maintain a rich choice of synonyms, observe the following differences in spelling and meaning. Use *forgo* to mean relinquish or do without (*to forgo the pleasure of your company*). Use *forego* to mean go before or precede (*the foregoing paragraph*); a *foregone conclusion* would be one that was arrived at beforehand.

foreword, forward: A *foreword* is a section of a book that precedes the main part; it's the one with *words* in it. The word *forward* means bold or presumptuous, as well as the opposite of backward.

Traditionally a *foreword* is written by someone other than the author, and what the author writes for the first part of a book is called a *preface*. However, *preface* and *foreword* are now widely accepted as synonyms.

formidable, impressive: Someone or something that is *formidable* (FOR-mi-dah-bull) arouses fear, dread, or alarm (*a formidable opponent*). If you want to convey respect or awe, use *impressive, convincing, imposing, touching,* or another adjective that fits.

fortnight: A period of two weeks.

fortuitous, fortunate: To be *fortuitous* is to happen without planning, by chance; to be *fortunate* is to be lucky.

> Their meeting at the airport was fortuitous.

> I was fortunate to have parents who often read to me.

An event can be both *fortuitous* and *fortunate*.

fourth estate: Journalists, the media.

fulsome: This adjective is defined as "offensively overdone, loathsome, or insincere" in some dictionaries, "full or abundant" in others. By not using the word, you avoid possible ambiguity.

fungible: Of such a nature that one unit or part can be substituted for an equivalent unit or part when discharging an obligation.

> Money and grain are fungible resources worldwide.

Gg

gamut, gantlet, gauntlet: *Gamut* suggests a complete range, as when someone experiences the whole gamut of emotions. *Gantlet* and *gauntlet* both derive from a challenge or a challenging situation. To *run the gantlet* is a military punishment requiring the accused to run between two lines of soldiers armed with sticks and knotted cords; *gauntlet* is a glove, traditionally thrown to the ground as a challenge to fight. Some dictionaries accept *gantlet* and *gauntlet* as alternative spellings, probably because of their common origin. But the distinction is a useful one—we might as well preserve it. In brief, you run a *gantlet* and throw down a *gauntlet*.

gemütlichkeit (Ger., guh-MOOT-likh-kiit): Homey feeling, cordiality.

gender, sex: *Gender*, a grammatical term, classifies parts of speech as masculine, feminine, or neuter; *sex* indicates male- or femaleness. Increasingly, however, as people tiptoe around the word *sex*, this distinction has all but disappeared. *Sex* now primarily refers to the sexual act or sexual activity, and *gender* has taken over as the word to use for identifying individuals as male or female; it is also used as an adjective (*gender politics*) where its use avoids a connotation of sexual activity.

genteelism: An expression used by someone who is trying, rather unsuccessfully, to appear refined.

genus, species: These two terms are part of the system of taxonomic classification that consists of kingdom, phylum, subphylum, class, order, family, genus, species, and subspecies. The human niche in this classification is the genus *Homo* (man) and the species *sapiens* (wise). Note that an initial capital letter is used with genus but not with species: *Homo sapiens*.

germane, material, relevant: Something that is pertinent to a given matter is *germane* or *relevant* (*a relevant point, a germane example*); if it is *material*, it is necessary as well (*a material witness*).

ODDS & ENDS

Near Misses: Look over the expressions in the left-hand column; if they look correct, you'd better study the correct version on the right.

WHAT WAS SAID	WHAT WAS MEANT
affidavid	affidavit
Cadillac converter	catalytic converter
carport tunnel	carpal tunnel
escape goat	scapegoat
gorilla warfare	guerilla warfare
insinnuendo	insinuate or innuendo
ivy tower	ivory tower
Klu Klux Klan	Ku Klux Klan
notary republic	notary public
overhauls	overalls
pacific	specific
proof is in the pudding	proof of the pudding is in the eating
radioactive increase	retroactive increase
safety deposit box	safe deposit box
seizure salad	Caesar salad
tender hooks	tenterhooks
use to	used to
verbage	verbiage
visa versa	vice versa

gerrymander: To draw the lines of a voting district so as to give unfair advantage to one party.

get, got: In formal writing, replace these informal verbs with a more specific verb.

> Informal: They got home late.

> Formal: They arrived home late.

gibe, jibe: To *gibe* is to heckle or taunt; to *jibe* (an informal term sometimes mispronounced "jive") is to agree with.

glasnost (Russ.): Openness, transparency (especially social and political).

good, well: Let's sort out these two words with a brief review of parts of speech. *Good* is an adjective (i.e., it modifies or describes a noun or pronoun); *well* is an adverb (i.e., it modifies a verb, adjective, or other adverb). Thus, when you are modifying a verb, use the adverb *well*.

> She played the piano well.

When you are modifying a noun, use the adjective *good*.

> She was a good pianist.

Well is also used to describe physical health: I feel well. "I feel good" is informal usage that adds an element of happiness or lightheartedness.

gourmand, gourmet, epicure: These words tweak aspects of food and drink and their enjoyment. *Gourmand* and *gourmet* are now treated by many dictionaries as synonymous, but a distinction can be maintained. A *gourmand* is one who delights in eating well and heartily; it occasionally implies gluttony, so use the word with care. *Gourmet* and *epicure* are synonyms for a connoisseur of fine food and drink.

grow: The transitive verb *grow* means to cultivate or raise, as one grows a crop. The use of *grow* with an abstraction (such as the economy) grates on the nerves of careful writers and speakers. Use *grow* to describe growing a moustache or an orchid, but not a business or the economy; these may indeed grow (i.e., become larger or stronger), but you don't grow them.

> The living wage program will stimulate the economy.

Hh

habeus corpus (Lat., "produce the body"): A court order that allows a prisoner to be brought before a judge so that he or she might be released from unlawful custody.

hail, hale: *Hail* is a noun meaning frozen rain (*a hailstorm*) and a verb meaning to greet or seek attention (*hail a taxi*). It is sometimes used figuratively (*his statement produced a hail of criticism*). The adjective *hale* means robust (*hale and hearty*); the verb *hale* means to force (*to hale into court*).

> What's worse than raining cats and dogs? Hailing taxis.

halcyon (HAL-see-ON) **days:** Carefree times.

hanged, hung: Use *hanged* for the act of executing someone by hanging; otherwise, use *hung* (the past tense of the verb *to hang*).

The room was cheerier after she had hung the curtains.

Hung is also an adjective meaning deadlocked (*a hung jury*).

hara-kiri: Japanese ritual suicide by disembowelment.

haute cuisine (Fr., oht kwee-ZEEN, "high cooking"): Refers to a top-of-the-line style of preparing food.

heighth: A non-word; use *height*.

historic, historical: *Historic* means of importance in history; it is overused in the media by those wishing to claim more importance for an event than is justified. *Historical* means pertaining to or concerned with history.

> The historical society was able to preserve the historic landmark.

> Passage of the bill was treated as a historic event.

The correct indefinite article to use with either word is *a*, not *an*.

Ghost: A game in which the first player calls out the first letter of a word consisting of three or more letters; the second player adds another letter that continues, but doesn't complete, a word. Continue until one player is forced to finish a word, thereby becoming one-third of a Ghost. Any player upon adding a letter can be challenged by the next player to say what the word will be; the person losing that challenge becomes one-third of a Ghost. The third such loss and the player is out of the game.

hoi polloi (Gr., "the masses," "the people"): *Hoi* means "the," so "the hoi polloi" is redundant.

⭐ **home, hone:** Frequently misused, these words have no roots or meaning in common. To seek a target is to *home* (*homing in on an objective, homing pigeon*); to sharpen is to *hone* (*honing skills*). The word *in* often follows *home*, but never *hone*.

⭐ **homogeneous, homogenous:** *Homogeneous* describes something that is uniform in structure or composition throughout. *Homogenous*, which often appears as a misspelling of *homogeneous*, is a biological term that indicates a correspondence between organs or parts in animals related by common descent, and is thus a word few of us need to use. Generally the word you want is *homogeneous*.

> The audience, a homogeneous group of retired civil servants, responded enthusiastically.

homograph, homonym, homophone: The key to sorting through these potentially confusing words is to notice their endings: *-graph* suggests writing, *-nym* suggests name, and *-phone* suggests sound. Thus, *homographs* are words with the same spelling (the same "writing") but different meanings and pronunciations (v., *lead*, pronounced LEED; n., *lead*, pronounced LED); *homonyms* are words with the same pronunciation and spelling (the same "names") but different meanings (n., *bear*, v., *bear*); *homophones* are words with the same pronunciation (the same "sound") but different spellings and meanings (*write, right*).

⭐ **hopefully:** *Hopefully* is an adverb that means full of hope.

> They contemplated the future hopefully.

It is sometimes used in place of *I hope*, thereby setting off alarm bells in some quarters.

Hopefully I will win the lottery.

You can sidestep this argument by avoiding the word.

Incendiary: Hopefully they will reach a settlement before the strike deadline.

Safe: They hope to reach a settlement.

hubris (HYEW-bris): Overweening pride. And what does *overweening* mean? Presumptuously arrogant; overbearing; excessive, immoderate. *Hubris* packs a lot into its six letters.

hyperbole (high-PURR-boh-lee): An exaggeration, sometimes deliberate (*I could have eaten a bushel of them*).

Ii

i.e. See E.G.

I, Me, Myself: The most common error associated with these pronouns is using *I* (the subjective case) when *me* (the objective case) is called for.

Riley invited Joe and me (*not* I) for dinner.

As the names imply, you should use the subjective case when the pronoun is the subject of a sentence or phrase, and the objective case when the pronoun is the object. This rule seems clear to about half the English-speaking population and is lost on the other half, despite their being advised to mentally remove *Joe and* from the phrase. If you're in the lost half, see BETWEEN YOU AND I (ME) and WHO, WHOM.

When *I* or *me* follows the word *than,* add the missing thought to help determine your choice.

Marisela loves Todd more than me.

Marisela loves Todd more than (she loves) me.

Marisela loves Todd more than I.

Marisela loves Todd more than I (love Todd).

Use *myself* only for emphasis (*I will pay the bill myself*) or when a reflexive verb is called for (*I injured myself*). Do not use it as a substitute for *I* or *me*.

Wrong: Julie and myself will be attending the meeting.

Right: Julie and I will be attending the meeting.

idée fixe (Fr., ee-DAA FEEKS, "fixed idea"): Obsession or fixation.

idiom: The translation of the Greek work *idios* from which *idiom* is derived is "a manifestation of the peculiar." That suggests the nature of an idiom, which is an expression peculiar to a given dialect, language, or area. Idioms are figurative expressions to which native speakers have become accustomed.

Let's hit the hay.

They were pushing the envelope.

You can't pull the wool over my eyes.

if, whether: These two conjunctions are often interchangeable. In general, choose the one that sounds right and whose meaning is clear.

> Let me know if you will be there.

Use *whether* when there's a choice between two alternatives (*I had trouble deciding whether to go to the first or second performance*) and when it precedes a noun clause (*Whether we would be late was uncertain*).

ilk: A noun meaning type or kind; loosely used (often disparagingly) to refer to a group of people of a certain kind or type.

> You can't rely on people of that ilk.

OED calls this usage erroneous, preferring the original meaning of *same*. In their view, *of that ilk* is properly used in *the Bostons of that ilk*, where it means the Bostons of Boston. The *OED* position appears to me to be a lonely one.

illegal, illicit: An *illegal* act is against the law; an *illicit* act is one that is not sanctioned by custom or moral code (*an illicit affair*), but is not necessarily against the law.

illegible, unreadable: Bad handwriting can result in an *illegible* (undecipherable) document.

> Do doctors take a course to learn how to write illegibly?

An *unreadable* document is one that is hard to understand because it is poorly written; a document that cannot be scanned by a machine is also called *unreadable*, though it may be quite legible.

Ragaman: And you thought Scrabble was challenging? Try Ragaman (the name is an anagram of *anagram*). A grid of blank squares is drawn (usually 5x5, 7x7, or 9x9). First player enters a letter in the center square. Second player adds a letter in one of the adjacent squares, to make a word or anagram. For example, if the first player writes *B*, the second can add *E* and score two points for the word *be*. Play continues, adding letters that make words or anagrams horizontally, vertically, or diagonally. Players score for each of the new words or anagrams made by their one letter, up to four words with one move (two diagonals plus a vertical and a horizontal). It makes me dizzy just thinking of it.

immigrate. See EMIGRATE.

imminent. See EMANATE.

impact: Although many language mavens have given up the fight against the widespread use of *impact* as a synonym for such words as *effect* and *influence*, those who still resist this usage feel strongly about it. They have a point. An *impact* is a violent coming together of two objects (e.g., when a meteorite hits the Earth's surface). To use *impact* to describe the effect of an increase in consumer prices dilutes its usefulness. Unless you are describing a physical effect, use words such as *effect* or *influence*.

impasse, stalemate: An *impasse*, though it indicates being stuck at the moment, suggests the possibility of alternative action. A *stalemate* is a deadlock.

impel. See COMPEL.

implicit. See EXPLICIT.

imply, infer: You *imply* when you hint at, insinuate, or suggest strongly; you *infer* when you deduce from evidence or draw a conclusion. Think of *imply* as a transmitting process and *infer* as a receiving process. Smoke often implies fire. When you smell the smoke, you infer that there's a fire.

impressive. See FORMIDABLE.

impromptu, extemporaneous: *Impromptu* remarks are made on the spur of the moment, in response to an immediate stimulus. *Extemporaneous* remarks, though they may be planned, are made without a written text or reference to notes.

in absentia (Lat., in ab-SEN-cha, "in absence"): While, or although, not present.

> They sent their greetings in absentia.

inamorata/inamorato (It.): The person with whom someone is enamored. The feminine form is *inamorata* and the masculine, *inamorato*.

> Steve is my current inamorato.

incipient, insipid: *Incipient* means just beginning to exist, or in an early state *(an incipient illness)*; *insipid* is boring, lacking in interest *(insipid remarks)*.

incommunicado (Sp.): Not reachable; without the means of communicating with others, as when one is held in solitary confinement.

★**incredible, incredulous:** These are the negative forms of *credible* and *credulous*. Results might be incredible, leading one to be incredulous. See also CREDIBLE.

indifferent. See DIFFIDENT.

ineffective, inefficient, ineffectual. See EFFECTIVE.

inexorable, inflexible: These adjectives both mean not capable of being swayed or diverted from a course. *Inexorable* describes forces (fate, the law) that are inevitable or uncompromising (the hurricane's inexorable path). *Inflexible* means unalterable or unbending *(inflexible rules)*.

infamous. See CELEBRATED.

infectious. See CONTAGION.

inflammable. See FLAMMABLE.

ingenious, ingenuous. See DISINGENUOUS.

initialism. See ABBREVIATION.

in loco parentis (Lat., in LOH-koh pah-REN-tis): In place of a parent.

>   The college functions in loco parentis for incoming students.

in medias res (Lat., in MAA-dee-ahs RAASS): In the middle of things.

★**insidious, invidious:** Something that is *insidious* spreads in a subtle or stealthy manner; it can be sly, treacherous, or beguiling *(an insidious leak to the press)*. Something that is *invidious* is offensive, tending to arouse ill will *(invidious remarks)*.

insincere. See DISINGENUOUS.

insure. See ASSURE.

inter-, intra-: The prefix *inter-* means between *(inter-city transit system)*; the prefix *intra-* means within *(intravenous injection)*.

inter alia (Lat.): Among other things.

> Pressing obligations were cited as one reason, inter alia, for not participating.

intercede, intervene: To *intercede* is to plead on another's behalf, to act as mediator in a dispute. To *intervene* is to come between two things or points of time.

intersect. See BISECT.

intuitive, instinctive: *Intuitive* means arising without conscious thought or analysis; *instinctive* is inborn, an innate aptitude. You might place a bet based on *intuition* and react to a loud noise *instinctively*.

in vino veritas (Lat., in VEE-noh VEHR-I-tahs, "in wine, truth"): An allusion to the fact that when under the influence of wine, people will say things they usually try to conceal.

ipso facto (Lat.): By the fact, thus. See also EX POST FACTO.

irony, sarcasm: *Irony* uses words to convey the opposite of their literal meaning—in other words, saying one thing but meaning another. It employs a deliberate contrast between apparent and intended meaning, an incongruity between what is expected and what happens. *Sarcasm* is used with the intent of ridiculing or scoring points, as in "You're all heart." The *irony* of the Jamaican bobsled team was not in their winning (they didn't), but simply in their existence. It provided Olympics commentators with rich opportunities for *sarcasm*.

irregardless: A non-word; it has one too many syllables. Use *regardless*.

irritate. See AGGRAVATE.

its, it's: When you want a possessive pronoun, use *its* (*The dog wagged its tail*). *It's* is a contraction of *it is* or *it has*. Using these words correctly is not just following a silly rule—they do mean different things. The cat and the mouse in the following example are aware of the difference.

> The cat sees its dinner. The mouse sees it's dinner.

Jj

jeremiad (Fr., JAIR-uh-MII-ad): A long lament.

jibe. See GIBE.

jihad (Arab., jee-hahd): Declaration of a holy war; a crusade. *Jihad* is also a metaphor for a holy war against evil within oneself; an inner cleansing or purification.

joie de vivre (Fr., zhwah deh VEE-vreh): Joy of life, a talent for living.

junta. See CABAL.

Kk

karat. See CARAT.

kudos (Gr., KYEW-dohs): Despite its appearance, *kudos* is a singular word (there is no "kudo"), and thus it takes a singular verb. However, since a singular verb with *kudos* looks so much like an error (as in *Kudos was long overdue*), I would probably substitute a word such as *acclaim* and reserve *kudos* for short, verbless expressions: Kudos to the author!

Ll

lagniappe (Louisiana Fr., lahn-yap): Something extra; a gratuity.

laissez-faire (Fr., LES-say FAIR, "allow [them] to do"): To let be, let go; an economic or political policy of letting things go their own course without intervention.

languid, limpid: These two adjectives are not synonyms. *Languid* means limp, lacking energy or vitality, listless; *limpid* means clear, calm, untroubled.

larceny. See BURGLARY.

laudable, laudatory: *Laudable* means praiseworthy *(a laudable effort)*; *laudatory* means expressing praise *(laudatory remarks)*.

lay, lie: Most of the problems associated with these two words can be resolved if you remember that *lay* (meaning to place) is a transitive verb (i.e., it takes an object) and *lie* (meaning to recline) is an intransitive verb (i.e., it doesn't take an object).

Lay the book on the table. (*Book* is the object of the transitive verb *lay*.)

I'm going to lie down for a few minutes. (The intransitive verb *lie* has no object.)

However, the past tense of *lie* is *lay*, and therein lies the confusion. Perhaps the following table will help:

VERB	PRESENT TENSE	PAST TENSE	EXAMPLE
to lay (to place)	lay	laid	Lay the wreath here. I laid the wreath on the grave.
to lie (to recline)	lie	lay	I'm going to lie down now. I lay down for a few minutes.
to lie (to prevaricate)	lie	lied	I don't lie when asked my age. She lied about her age.

Another meaning of the verb *lie*, to reside in, is not usually a source of error.

The strength of a nation lies in the homes of its people.
—Abraham Lincoln

lebensraum (Ger., LAY-bens-raum, "living space"): The Nazi excuse given for invading Poland in 1939 was their need for *lebensraum*.

legend. See ALLEGORY.

le mot juste (Fr., leh moh jhoost): Exactly the right word; the only one.

lend, loan: Many authorities acknowledge that the noun *loan* has essentially replaced the verb *lend*. I prefer to retain both words, however. "Loan me your ears"? Never!

> Please lend me your pen.

> The bank is lending us the money to buy a house.

> We went to the bank for a loan.

less. See FEWER.

lethologica: Inability to recall the right word. Also known as a "senior moment." When experiencing this condition, you may insert the word *whoozis* and proceed with whatever you were saying. By the time you reach the end of the sentence, you may have remembered the word, or someone will have provided it. In any case, your meaning will probably be clear.

liable. See APT.

libel, slander: Whether defamatory remarks are written or spoken determines their classification as libel or slander. To qualify as *libel*, the remarks must be both written and published; spoken defamatory remarks are *slander*. In either case, the words must be inaccurate and potentially damaging to the person's reputation or career to be grounds for legal action.

like. See AS.

likely. See APT.

lingua franca (It., LING-gwa FRAHN-kah, "the Frankish tongue"): A common language used by people who speak different languages.

> English is the lingua franca of the U.N.

Also, a hybrid language (Italian, French, Spanish, Greek, and Turkish) spoken in the Mediterranean region.

literally. See FIGURATIVELY.

literati (It., lih-ter-RAH-tee): The literary intelligentsia.

livid, lurid: *Livid* means bluish (as in a bruise), rather than the popular misconception of reddish. "Being very angry" is a meaning that's accepted by some dictionaries, but the *OED* calls such usage colloquial. *Lurid* refers to something that shocks because of its sensationalism or unsavory qualities, despite also meaning pallid, sallow in color. *Lurid details* is a cliché.

loath, loathe: *Loath* is an adjective meaning reluctant (*I am loath to depart*); *loathe* is a verb meaning despise (*I loathe the thought of it*).

loose, lose: The difference in pronunciation of these two words is important. *Loose* (adj., loos) means unfastened; *lose* (v., looz) means to be unable to find, to be deprived of; it is the antonym of win, gain, or find.

lumpenproletariat (Ger.): A disenfranchised group.

luxuriant, luxurious: *Luxuriant* means profuse, growing abundantly (*a luxuriant patch of weeds*); *luxurious* means offering sumptuous pleasure or comfort, at a price (*a luxurious lifestyle*).

majority, plurality: At least half of the votes plus one is a *majority;* when there are three or more candidates, the largest number of votes is a *plurality*. Whether *majority* is singular or plural depends on whether the group representing the majority is viewed as a unified whole or as individuals.

> The majority of the country opposes war. (singular)

> The majority were late in filing their returns. (plural)

In a sentence such as "He spent the majority of his time . . . ," replace *the majority* with *most*. Reserve *majority* for the larger of two clearly distinguishable entities. *Majority* also refers to legal adulthood.

malapropism: A humorous misuse of words, whether intentionally or in ignorance: "shrewd awakening" instead of "rude awakening." Named after Mrs. Malaprop, a character in Sheridan's play *The Rivals*. She liked to use big words but didn't know their meaning (e.g., the "geometry of contagious countries").

mammon: Money or wealth, which was regarded in the New Testament as an evil influence when it becomes a preoccupation or object of worship; thus, generally, such an evil influence.

marginal: Use *marginal* to describe something falling near a lower limit; a marginal enterprise would be one that's struggling to stay alive. *Marginal* is often used when *small* or *slight* is what's actually meant; change *a marginal difference* to *a slight difference*.

marine, maritime, nautical, naval: The noun *marine* refers to a member of the U.S. Marine Corps; the adjective *marine* means relating to the sea. *Maritime* describes lands bordering the sea or refers to shipping or navigation on the sea. *Naval* and *nautical* used to be synonyms, but *naval* now has a more restricted meaning, referring to the personnel and ships of a navy (a military sea force); *nautical* is the more general term, referring to anything relating to sailors, ships, and navigation.

marital, marshal, martial: *Marital* means of or pertaining to marriage; a simple transposition of two letters produces *martial*, which means of or pertaining to war. (No comment.) They are derived from unrelated words. The noun *marshal* (note that the word is spelled with one *l*) refers to a military rank (field marshal), to someone who leads a parade, or to an officer who carries out a court order; the verb *marshal* means to arrange or set in methodical order, to enlist and organize (*to marshal your resources*).

material, materiel: *Material* (mah-TEER-ee-ul) is the substance out of which something is made; *materiel* (mah-teer-ee-EL) refers to supplies needed in any undertaking (though most frequently used in a military context). See also GERMANE.

matrix (MAA-triks): Outside of its legitimate mathematical use (a rectangular array of symbols), *matrix* is a faddish word meaning something like a womb or mold in which something is engendered. See also PARADIGM.

maven (Yid., MAA-ven, "understanding"): An individual who is knowledgeable or experienced about a given subject.

may. See CAN.

me. See I, ME, MYSELF.

mea culpa (Lat., MAY-ah KUL-pah, "I am culpable"): I am at fault. Usually accompanied by a certain amount of breast-beating.

mean, median. See AVERAGE.

meantime, meanwhile: The noun *meantime* refers to an interval, the time between one occurrence and another; thus it is appropriate to say "in the meantime." The adverb *meanwhile* means during an interval, thus rendering "in the meanwhile" redundant. Either say "in the meantime" or "meanwhile."

media, medium: *Media* is the plural form of *medium*, which means a channel of mass communication, a substance used in laboratories to cultivate microorganisms, a person claiming to communicate with the dead, and a form for artistic expression. Careful writers treat *medium* as singular and *media* as plural.

> The media are (*not* is) sometimes confrontational.

> Television is occasionally a medium of communication.

The plural *mediums* is appropriate when referring to persons or to the laboratory substance. (For other irregular plurals, see *Write Right!*)

meet, mete: The adjective *meet* (which *AHD* classifies as archaic) means suitable, proper. The verb *mete* means to deal out, to allot; the noun means limit, boundary.

It is meet to mete out punishment under the circumstances.

memento: A souvenir. NOTE: Though some dictionaries list *momento* as a variant spelling of *memento*, most language authories consider *momento* to be an error. In my book, it's a non-word. Think *re<u>mem</u>brance*.

memento mori (Lat.): A reminder of mortality.

ménage à trois (Fr., may-NAHJH ah TRWAH): An intimate combination of three people.

mensch (Yid. "man"): A person who does the right, generous thing.

meretricious, meritorious: *Meretricious* means lacking sincerity *(a meretricious argument)*; attracting attention in a vulgar way *(a meretricious display)*; pertaining to or resembling a prostitute. *Meritorious* is having merit; deserving reward or praise *(meritorious behavior)*. Be careful to use these words correctly, in view of their contrasting meanings.

metaphor, simile: A metaphor is a figure of speech in which two things are not so much compared as made identical. I speak metaphorically when I suggest that *The Right Word!* is a toolkit. Metaphoric language includes expressions such as *fueling the economy*, *launching a website*, and *anchoring a panel discussion*. Shakespeare created a *mixed metaphor* when Hamlet pondered whether he should "take arms against a sea of troubles." Not all mixed metaphors are so successful.

A *simile* (SIM-i-lee) uses the words *like* or *as* to compare two dissimilar things.

Errors sprout like dandelions.

He was as mad as a rooster in an empty henhouse.

meteor, meteorite, meteoroid: *Meteoroids* consist of pieces of galactic debris floating through space. When a piece of the debris enters Earth's atmosphere, it is called a *meteor* (a shooting star). A piece that survives the fall to Earth is called a *meteorite*.

miasma (mii-AZ-mah): Poisonous atmosphere or emanations; thus, any noxious influence.

militate, mitigate: To *militate* is to operate against something; to *mitigate* is to assuage or make more endurable.

His stiff demeanor militated against his wish to appear friendly.

They suggested several ways to mitigate environmental damage.

mnemonic (Gr., neh-MON-ik, from *mneme*, "memory"): A device for assisting memory (as the *e* in *letter* serves as a reminder for the correct spelling of *stationery*). Related words are *amnesia* and *amnesty*.

model, paradigm, paragon (n.): *Model* is an example of a high standard of behavior; a scaled-down version of some object (e.g., a jetliner); a preliminary pattern for an item to be built (e.g., an automobile); or a complex of phenomena to be studied (e.g., weather). A *paradigm* is an exhaustive model, one that aims to omit no detail. See also PARADIGM. A *paragon* is a model of excellence, an ideal that may be approached.

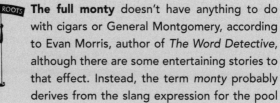

The full monty doesn't have anything to do with cigars or General Montgomery, according to Evan Morris, author of *The Word Detective*, although there are some entertaining stories to that effect. Instead, the term *monty* probably derives from the slang expression for the pool of money at stake in the card game *monte* (Spanish for "mountain"). It's not too much of a leap to go from "the full monty" to "the whole shebang," which is the current meaning of the expression.

modus operandi (Lat.): Method or way of operating; abbreviated m.o.

modus vivendi (Lat.): Way of living.

momento: A non-word. See MEMENTO.

moot. See ACADEMIC.

moral, morale: The adjective *moral* relates to matters of right and wrong; ethical. The noun *morale* refers to individual or group attitude, such as enthusiasm or cooperativeness.

> They took a moral position regarding the honor code.

> Morale was high when the team entered the competition.

morbidity, mortality: Disease or lack of health are instances of *morbidity; mortality* refers to the state of being subject to death (i.e., not immortal).

> Our mortality is evident when I consider the morbidity rates associated with certain diseases.

mountebank: A spectacular charlatan.

mutual. See COMMON.

★ **myriad:** A large number. Write "myriad examples," not "a myriad of examples."

myself. See I, ME, MYSELF.

myth. See ALLEGORY.

Nn

nabob (Port., NAA-bob): A man of wealth and power.

nadir, zenith: *Nadir* (NAA-der) is the lowest point; *zenith* (ZEE-nith), the highest point.

nano-: A prefix that means one billionth (one part in a billion). The current interest in nanotechnology may be why *nano-* is now overused in other contexts to indicate a very small amount (*I hesitated for a nanosecond*). Let's leave this prefix to the nanotechnologists.

★ **nauseated, nauseous:** When you feel sick, you are *nauseated*. What makes you feel sick is *nauseous* (*a nauseous stench*).

nebbish (Yid.): A timid, weak person.

nefarious, multifarious: *Nefarious* means evil or infamous. *Multifarious* means having great variety; made up of many parts or kinds.

nihilism (NII-il-izm): A doctrine or belief that nothing exists or can be communicated, that moral principles have no objective ground and life is meaningless.

nirvana (Sans., neer-VAH-nah, "extinction"): State of complete blessedness; ideal condition of harmony and bliss.

noblesse oblige (Fr., noh-BLESS oh-BLEEJ, "nobility obligates"): Noble or honorable behavior considered to be the obligation of one of nobility or rank.

noisome: Noxious, smelly, nasty; it does not mean noisy.

noli me tangere (Lat., NOH-lee mee TAN-jer-ree, "do not touch me"): A warning not to meddle, touch, or interfere.

nolo contendere (Lat., NOH-low con-TEN-dir-ree, "I do not wish to contend"): A defendant's plea in a criminal case; although this plea is equivalent to an admission of guilt in terms of punishment, it allows a defendant to deny charges in a future case.

nom de plume (Fr.): A pen name. Mark Twain was the nom de plume of Samuel Clemens.

none: Not any, no one, nobody. The troublesome aspect of this pronoun is whether it is singular or plural. Use a singular verb when *none* means no one or not one or when it precedes a singular noun (*None of the money was returned*). Use a plural verb when *no persons* can be substituted for *none* (*None are more overworked than single parents*). If *none* can be logically construed as either singular or plural, take your pick.

None of the board members is (*or* are) available for comment.

non sequitur (Lat., "it does not follow"): An inference or conclusion that does not follow from established premises or evidence.

To assume that I am not well informed because I don't watch television is a non sequitur.

nota bene (Lat., NOH-tah BAA-naa): Note well; often added as a caution. Abbreviated N.B.

notorious. See CELEBRATED.

nuclear: The word *nuclear* is pronounced noo-klee-ur, *not* noo-kyew-lur.

number. See AMOUNT.

Oo

obscene: An adjective that originally stressed lewdness or indecency, especially with respect to standards of morality. *OED* has restored the word to a broader usage: offensive to the senses; disgusting, repulsive, filthy, loathsome. Stonings or the

Vietnam War might be described as *obscene* by those adopting this interpretation of the word. Kingsley Amis protested this "hijacking" of the word:

> *What we have seen is much less the restoration to general use of a somewhat archaic sense* [of obscene] *than the impious and impudent hijacking or bagging of a word for sensationalist purposes. . . . Dreadful things happen in the world all the time. . . . These are not grossly indecent or lewd; in a word they are not what we have nowadays come to understand by* obscene, *however disgusting and depraved they may be.*

I'm with Amis. Let's reserve this adjective for lewd or indecent circumstances.

obsolescent, obsolete: *Obsolete* means no longer used or useful; *obsolescent* means becoming obsolete.

obstinate, stubborn: The adjective *obstinate* indicates inflexibly adhering to an opinion or course of action; resistant to reason. The characteristic of inflexibility is common to both *obstinate* and *stubborn*, but *obstinate* has a negative connotation while *stubborn* can be viewed as an admirable quality.

> She stubbornly refused to cut corners.

> Her obstinate refusal to listen to further arguments hampered the negotiations.

obviate. See ELIMINATE.

omertà (It.): The code of secrecy and silence in the Sicilian mafia.

onomatopeia (Gr., ahn-oh-mah-toe-PEE-ya): A term that sounds like what it refers to *(hiss, pop)*.

opaque, translucent, transparent: These three adjectives relate to how well materials transmit light. *Opaque* means impenetrable by light; *translucent* means transmitting light but with enough diffusion to prevent objects from being seen clearly; *transparent* means transmitting light so that objects are clearly visible.

opportunistic, pragmatic: An *opportunistic* individual is one who seizes opportunities or takes advantage of a situation without regard for the consequences; a *pragmatic* individual is governed by reason or practical considerations rather than theory.

oral, verbal: Confusion regarding these two words could be costly if it involves a contract. *Oral* means of or pertaining to the mouth; thus, an *oral agreement* is spoken rather than written. *Verbal* is less precise than *oral;* although it indicates by word of mouth, *verbal* can refer not only to what is expressed in speech but also in writing. To avoid confusion, request a *written* agreement.

ordinance, ordnance: An *ordinance* is a regulation or statute. *Ordnance* is military weaponry, together with the ammunition and equipment needed to keep them in good repair.

orient, orientate, orientation: To *orient* is to align or position with respect to a reference point. *Orientate* is a clumsy back formation; instead, use the verb *orient* or the noun *orientation*.

The instructions were to orient the pool so it could receive maximum sunshine.

The orientation of the pool allowed it to receive maximum sunshine.

otiose (OH-shee-ohs): Having a lazy nature; serving no useful purpose; ineffective. A handy invective.

outré (Fr., oo-TRAY, "beyond"): Bizarre, eccentric.

oxymoron: A concise contradiction in terms, such as legally drunk, tight slacks, and plastic glasses.

Pp

pail, pale: The noun *pail* refers to a bucket. The adjective *pale* means having a low intensity of color; wan. The verb *pale* means to turn pale, to diminish, to be outshone.

My editing skills pale beside those of my daughter.

palate, pallet, palette: *Palate* is the roof of the mouth; thus, something that appeals to the palate would relate to one's sense of taste *(palatable food)*. A *pallet*, among other meanings, refers to a narrow bed and a wooden platform used for storing and moving objects. A *palette* is a thin panel (often with thumb hole) on which an artist lays and mixes paints.

palpable, tactile, tangible: *Palpable* means capable of being felt, easily perceived, obvious *(a palpable sense of relief)*.

Use *tactile* when you're referring to the sense of touch *(tactile stimulation)*; use *tangible* for something concrete or real *(tangible proof)*.

panacea, remedy: A *panacea* (pan-uh-SEE-a) is a cure for all woes. *Remedy* is something that relieves pains, cures a disease, or corrects a disorder; in a legal context, *remedy* refers to a means of preventing or correcting a wrong or enforcing a right.

panache (Fr., pah-NAHSH): Flair, verve, style; literally, feathers, especially a plume on a hat.

paparazzi (Ital.): Opportunistic photojournalists.

parable. See ALLEGORY.

A **palindrome** is a word, phrase, verse, or sentence that reads the same forward or backward.

Sex at noon taxes.

A variation is called an **invertogram,** which reads the same right side up or down: dollop. (Well, it's close.)

paradigm (PEAR-a-DIME): An exhaustive model, example, or pattern. Peter Bowler *(The Superior Person's Book of Words)* has some advice about this pretentious word:

> Never use this word yourself, but be prepared, when it is used by another, to lean forward intently, narrow your eyes and say, "Just a moment—do you really **mean** paradigm *in that* context?" When somewhat bemused, he avers that he does, you merely raise your eyebrows and remain silent. With any luck at all, he will now have forgotten what he was going to say. Apply the same technique when confronted with parameter, infrastructure, structure, *and* matrix.

See also MODEL.

parameter, perimeter: *Parameter* is a variable or arbitrary constant appearing in a mathematical expression. It also refers to any of a set of physical properties whose values determine the characteristics or behavior of something (age, for example). It is not a synonym for *perimeter,* which is the line around an area *(the perimeter of a circle).*

WORD PLAY

A **pangram** is a sentence that incorporates all the letters of the alphabet. The shorter the sentence, the better. But so far, the closer they are to 26 letters, the more nonsensical they become. Here are some of the better ones.

Doxy with charming buzz quaffs vodka julep. (36 letters)

Pack my box with five dozen liquor jugs. (32)

Few quips galvanized the mock jury box. (32)

Quick zephyrs blow, vexing daft Jim. (29)

pari passu (Lat., pah-ree pah-soo): With equal application to; fairly; side by side.

We worked on both projects pari passu.

parlay, parley: *Parlay* is a verb meaning to maneuver to great advantage, often using one gain to create another. The verb *parley* means to discuss or debate, as with an enemy; the noun *parley* means a discussion or conference, especially between enemies over the terms of a truce or agreement.

pas de deux (Fr., PAH deh DYEU): Ballet dance for two.

pastiche (Fr., pa-STEESH): Hodgepodge.

patois (Fr., pa-twah): Special jargon or dialect of a given people.

peak, peek, pique: The top of a mountain is its *peak*; to glance quickly, especially from a concealed place, is to *peek*. The noun *pique* means a feeling of resentment that arises from wounded pride *(He stomped out of the room in a fit of pique)*; the verb *pique* means to arouse or spur *(The hint piqued my curiosity)*.

pedal, peddle: A *pedal* is a lever or other device operated by the foot (as on a bicycle or piano). The verb *peddle* means to sell, especially in small quantities; to travel about selling.

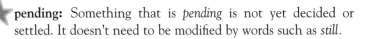

pending: Something that is *pending* is not yet decided or settled. It doesn't need to be modified by words such as *still*.

people, persons: Use *people* when referring to a large group of individuals collectively; use *persons* when referring to a specific and relatively small number of individuals.

Six persons were injured.

The people took to the streets.

perennial. See ANNUAL.

perquisite, prerequisite, requisite: A *perquisite* is an additional benefit coming from a job; its informal abbreviation is *perk*. *Prerequisite* is both a noun and an adjective that means a prior condition that must be fulfilled (*A prerequisite of the class is knowing how to speak Spanish*). *Requisite* means necessary, essential (*She has the requisite skills*).

per se (Lat., purr SAA): By itself, intrinsically.

His argument was correct, per se, but nonetheless insufficient.

persecute, prosecute: To *persecute* is to harass or annoy persistently, often because of race, religion, or political persuasion. To *prosecute* is to take legal action against someone or to conduct court proceedings. You might decide to prosecute someone who is persecuting you.

persona non grata (Lat.): Unwelcome person, someone out of favor.

perspicacity, perspicuity: *Perspicacity* refers to acuteness of perception or understanding; *perspicuity* is the quality of being clearly presented or easily understood.

Her ability to work well with troubled children revealed a rare level of perspicacity.

His perspicuity helped us arrive at a decision.

A **variation of the pangram** packs every letter of the alphabet into a limerick instead of a sentence. Here are a couple from a practitioner of this art, Neita Farmer.

The lady with extravagant ways
May justly be censored or praised
    With each shopping quest
    She zooms back redressed,
The GNP figure is raised.

Our history is full of great men
Some adept with knife, brush, or pen
    Very few can exist
    Who calmly persist
In just quietly practicing Zen.

persuade. See CONVINCE.

peruse, scan: To *peruse* is to read or examine carefully. *Scan* can mean either a quick look or close scrutiny—the context is supposed to alert the reader to which one:

> I started the day with a careful scanning of the want ads.

> A quick scan of the headlines was all that I had time for.

phase. See FAZE.

philistine (FIL-es-STEEN): An ignorant, uncultured person.

pièce de résistance (Fr., pee-ESS deh raa-zees-STAHns): The principal dish of a meal; an outstanding accomplishment.

pied à terre (Fr., pee-YAA dah TAIR, "a foot on earth"): A small apartment or office that isn't one's primary residence or place of business.

pivotal, vital: Although both words convey a sense of importance, use *pivotal* only to indicate something that is crucial to the outcome *(a pivotal decision)*. Use *vital* if you simply mean important or essential *(It is vital that you be there)*.

plausible. See FALLACIOUS.

pleonasm, redundancy, tautology: All three mean using more words than necessary, but the needless repetition of the synonyms *redundancy* and *tautology* usually comes from ignorance or carelessness.

> **Wrong:** It was déjà vu all over again.

A *pleonasm*, on the other hand, intentionally uses repetition in order to achieve an effect.

> Everyone, both rich and poor, was represented.

plethora (Lat., PLEH-thor-rah): A *plethora* is not merely a large quantity but a superabundance, an excess.

polemic: A controversy or argument, especially one that refutes an attack upon a specific position; also, a person inclined to argue or refute.

pore, pour: What you do with a document is *pore* over it (read or scrutinize intently); what you do with wine is *pour* it. Our skin has *pores* (minute surface openings).

possible, practicable, practical. See FEASIBLE.

practically, virtually: Use *practically* to mean in a practical manner, rather than as a substitute for *almost*. A more precise term for *almost* is *virtually*.

> Practically speaking, I may be unable to complete the manuscript in time.

> The California condor was virtually extinct.

pragmatic. See OPPORTUNISTIC.

precede, proceed: To *precede* (note the spelling) is to come before in time; to be in a position in front of; to go in advance of. To *proceed* is to continue, to go forward, especially after an interruption; to move on in an orderly way.

> Her arrival preceded mine by two hours.

> Let's proceed with the rest of the agenda.

precedence, precedents: If something takes *precedence*, it has priority over something else. *Precedents* are actions or words that are later referred to as justification for subsequent actions.

precipitate, precipitous: A *precipitate action* is hasty, possibly foolhardy. *Precipitous* is used primarily to indicate physical steepness (*a precipitous path*).

predicament. See DILEMMA.

predicated on: Many view this as a pompous way of saying "based on." I'm inclined to agree.

predominant, predominate: The adjective *predominant* means most common, prevalent (*the predominant color*). The verb *predominate* means to have controlling influence, to prevail (*Those in favor of the motion predominated*). *Predominantly* is the correct adverbial form, not *predominately* (even though it appears in some dictionaries).

prerequisite. See PERQUISITE.

prescribe, proscribe: To *prescribe* is to recommend a remedy, both in a medical and a more general context; to *proscribe* is to prohibit.

> A physician who prescribes particular medications may proscribe certain activities.

presently: Despite the "present" in *presently*, the word does not mean now; it means in a while, soon, shortly.

presumptive, presumptuous: *Presumptive* describes something that provides a reasonable basis for belief or acceptance; *presumptuous* means arrogant, excessively forward.

> The presumptive evidence suggested that the defendant's actions were presumptuous but not illegal.

prevent. See FORBID.

preventative: Use *preventive*. The meaning is the same: that which prevents or keeps from happening (*preventive medicine*). But *preventive* is more concise and elegant than *preventative*.

prima facie (Lat., PRII-mah FAA-shee, "on first appearance"): At first sight; before closer inspection.

principal, principle: *Principal* has both a noun and an adjective form; the noun refers to the head of a school or firm, or to capital that can earn interest; the adjective means leading or chief (*the principal reason for action*). *Principle* has only a noun form; it means rule or standard of conduct: *standing on principle* (*not* principal, as the tongue-in-cheek illustration on p. 16 humorously depicts).

> Both principal and interest had accrued in a special account; it was their principal source of income.

> The school principal is a person of strict principles.

problematic, troublesome: That which is *problematic* is difficult or open to debate; something *troublesome* is trying, worrisome, causing trouble.

pro bono (Lat., proh BOH-noh, "for the good"): Free legal services.

prodigal: *Prodigal* describes someone who is extravagant or excessively wasteful. It does not suggest wandering.

proficient. See ADEPT.

pro forma (Lat., "according to form"): Done as habitually done, according to form.

 **WORD ROOTS** Some tales of word origins make a good story but have little to do with the facts. According to the *American Heritage Dictionary*, the source of the word **pumpernickel** is the early New High German *pumpern* (fart) + *nickel* (devil), a pejorative so named from the bread's being hard to digest. However, the folk tale that lives on (perhaps as a euphemism) is that Napoleon tasted some German bread, didn't like it, and fed it to his horse, saying "Bon pour Nicole," hence, *pumpernickel.*

prohibit. See FORBID.

prone, prostrate, supine: All indicate lying down. *Prone* is face down, *supine* is face up; *prostrate* suggests collapsing, being thrown or throwing oneself down into the position, which can be either face down or up. See also APT, PROSTATE.

You must be p̲rone to do a p̲ush-up, s̲upine to do a s̲it-up.

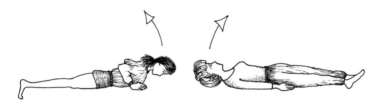

prophecy, prophesy: *Prophecy* (PRAH-fuh-see) is a noun meaning prediction. *Prophesy* (PRAH-fuh-SII) is a verb that means to forecast, to predict. (Note the difference in pronunciation of the last syllable.)

When you prophesy, you make a prophecy.

proportional, proportionate: Both adjectives convey the idea of being in proportion to something. *Proportional* is the better fit when it immediately precedes a noun (*proportional representation*); otherwise, use *proportionate* (*punishment proportionate to the crime*).

prostate: A part of the male anatomy; do not confuse the word with *prostrate*. See also PRONE.

protagonist. See ANTAGONIST.

Occupational Hazards: If monarchs are sometimes deposed and members of the clergy defrocked, would it follow that:

- exterminators are debugged
- dry cleaners are depressed
- electricians are delighted
- cowboys are deranged
- musicians are denoted
- underwear manufacturers are debriefed
- baseball players are debased
- politicians are devoted

Or how about these:

- the mathematician whose days are numbered
- the lawyer who has lost his will to live
- the auctioneer who is being bid a final farewell
- the dowser who is surrounded by well wishers

protocol: *Protocol* refers to the forms of ceremony and etiquette observed by diplomats and heads of state. It is also an outline to be followed in an experiment.

proximity: A noun meaning closeness or the state of being near. Thus, "close proximity" is redundant.

> Pottery shards were found in the proximity of the burial mound.

pusillanimous (pyew-si-LAN-ih-mus): Faint-hearted; marked by cowardice. This word is particularly appealing to adolescents looking for multisyllabic epithets.

putative (PEW-tah-tiv): Generally regarded as such; reputed.

putsch (Ger., "thrust"): An attempted coup.

Qq

quality: Using *quality* as an adjective has become popular in informal usage (*quality time with the kids*), but you should avoid it in formal writing, maybe even in informal use. *Quality* is correctly used as a noun meaning characteristic or attribute (*the quality of mercy*) or degree of excellence (*a fabric of low quality*).

question: Resist the temptation to tack on "as to" or "of" following this word.

The question whether we would attend was unresolved.

quidnunc (Lat., "what now"): A gossip, busybody.

quid pro quo (Lat., "something for something"): An equal exchange, tit for tat.

quixotic (kwik-SAH-tik): An adjective referring to the character in Cervantes' novel *Don Quixote* who had lofty but impractical ideals; generally a romantic individual who is not concerned with practicality. Reserve *quixotic* for such characters, not just to indicate eccentric, freakish, or disordered behavior.

quod erat demonstrandum (Lat., kwohd er-raht dem-ohn-STRAN-dum, "which was to be demonstrated"): Abbreviated Q.E.D. This abbreviation is put at the end of a mathematical proof to indicate that something that was to have been shown has indeed been shown. Also used when making a similar claim following presentation of a proposition or thesis.

quotation, quote: *Quotation* is a noun, and *quote* is a verb; they are not interchangeable.

> She closed with a quotation (*not* quote) from the Koran.

> May I quote you?

quotidian (Lat., kwoh-TID-dee-uhn): Everyday, occurring daily, ordinary.

Rr

rack, wrack: Chances are the word you're looking for is *rack*, which means to put under a strain, to torment (*nerve-racking, rack your brain*). *Wrack* is an archaic variant of *wreck* and mostly appears in the cliché *wrack and ruin*.

raison d'être (Fr.): Reason for being.

ravage, ravish: These verbs are not interchangeable. To *ravage* is to lay waste. To *ravish* is to enrapture, to carry away by force, but it also means to rape. Theodore Bernstein cites the erroneous use of *ravish* in the headline "Elm Beetle Infestation Ravishing Thousands of Trees." His comment: "Keep your mind on your work, buster."

realpolitic (Ger., RAY-al-POL-i-tik, "realistic politics"): Single-minded, tough political style.

realtor: This word is pronounced REE-ull-ter, not REE-li-ter. The trademark *Realtor* should be capitalized.

rebut. See DISPUTE.

recapitulate, reiterate, repeat: To *recapitulate* is to repeat in concise form, to review; it has a stilted flavor, as does to *reiterate*, which is a formal way of saying "to say again." Consider using *repeat*, which means to say or do something again.

reciprocal. See COMMON.

recto, verso (Lat.): *Recto* refers to a right-hand page, *verso* to a left-hand page *(the back side of a recto)*. The title page verso is the page on the back of the title page.

recur, reoccur: *Recur* means to come up again or repeatedly, to come to mind. "Reoccur" is a non-word.

red herring: A false clue.

redolent: Having or emitting fragrance; smelling.

reductio ad absurdum (Lat., reh-DUK-tee-oh ahd ahb-SUR-dum): Reduction to absurdity in order to show that a proposition is absurd when followed to its logical conclusion.

redundancy. See PLEONASM.

reek, wreak, wreck: To *reek* is to be permeated with a strong and unpleasant odor. To *wreak* is to inflict punishment or pain, usually in the context of revenge. It's what one does with havoc (not "wrecking havoc"). The noun *wreck* is something or someone who is in a shattered, broken-down state.

refute. See DISPUTE.

regime, regimen: Though there is some overlap here, *regime*
more often refers to a system of government (*during Napoleon's
regime*), and *regimen* to a system of therapy (*a regimen of diet
and exercise*).

regretfully, regrettably: *Regretfully* means with regret. *Regrettably* means unfortunately. The words are not interchangeable.

> The regrettable incident means that I must regretfully sub-
> mit my resignation.

Reversible words, cousins of palindromes, can be read in both directions, but as different words.

deliver/reviled

drawer/reward

desserts/stressed

straw/warts

reign, rein, rain: *Reign* refers to the exercise of sovereign power or to the period during which such power is exercised. The term is also applied generally to dominance or widespread influence.

The reign of Queen Victoria lasted more than half a century.

You pull or relax *reins* (leather straps) to control the speed and direction of a horse. Thus, to *rein in* is to slow or stop, while to *give free rein to* is to remove such restraints.

The Federal Reserve Board tried to rein in inflation.

Rain is the wet stuff that falls from the sky.

relegate. See DELEGATE.

relevant. See GERMANE.

reluctant, reticent: To be *reluctant* is to be unwilling; to be *reticent* is to be reluctant to speak.

remedy. See PANACEA.

repel, repulse: Something that *repels* you is distasteful; it may make you feel squeamish. To *repulse* is to drive back, as you might an enemy attack.

replete. See COMPLETE.

repudiate. See DISPUTE.

requisite. See PERQUISITE.

respectively: This adverb means singly, in the order designated. Do not use *respectively* as the closing salutation for a letter (that should be *respectfully*).

revenge. See AVENGE.

rictus: An expanse of open mouth, as in the fixed gaping of a corpse.

robbery. See BURGLARY.

roman à clef (Fr., row-MAHN ah KLAA, "novel with a key"): Novel in which characters are modeled on real people.

root, rout, route: The below-ground part of a plant is its *root*; it's also what you do for the home team. *Rout* (rhymes with *snout*) is an overwhelming defeat (in other words, what you hope happens to the other team). *Route* (rhymes with *snoot*) is the road you travel to reach the game.

Ss

salad days: Lost youth or naïveté; one of Shakespeare's many coinages.

sang-froid (Fr., sahng frwah, "cold blood"): Fearlessness, stoic calm.

sardonic: Means scornful or mocking and can refer to content (*sardonic humor*) or manner of delivery (*sardonic smile*).

savoir faire (Fr.): To know how to do things. That quality we all hope to have.

scan. See PERUSE.

schadenfreude (Ger., SHAHD-en-FROID-eh): Joy in someone's misfortune.

scenario: Strictly speaking, a *scenario* is a plot outline or script. Its widespread popularity as a projected sequence of events has turned it into a cliché (*worst-case scenario*).

scrimp, skimp: Both verbs suggest being extremely sparing. To *scrimp* is to economize severely; to *skimp* is to do something hastily or with poor materials.

> To scrimp on her weekly food budget, she had to skimp on some of the soup ingredients.

semi-. See BI-.

seraphim. See CHERUBIM.

sesquipedalian (Lat., SES-kwa-pa-DAA-lyun, "one and a half feet"): Words that are extra long. A lake in Massachusetts named Chargoggpagoggmanchauggagoggchaubunagungaamaugg takes sesquipedalianism to a new level; a rough translation is "You fish on your side, I fish on my side, nobody fishes in the middle."

ODDS & ENDS

Scrabble (originally called "It," and then "Criss-Cross") was invented during the Depression by an unemployed architect named Alfred Butts. A friend came up with the name Scrabble and sold 2,000 of the games; one of the customers was the owner of Macy's. The rest, as they say, is history.

But did you know that if you can work the word "psychoanalyzing" into a game, you will add as much as 1,539 points to your score. The highest point score possible, so I'm told, is 4,153.

sewage, sewerage: *Sewage* is the liquid and solid waste carried off by sewers. *Sewerage* refers to the system of underground pipes that constitutes a sewer.

sex. See GENDER.

shall/will, should/would: Fifty years ago, Wilson Follett (author of *Modern American Usage*) devoted 23 pages to *shall* and *will*; today, the rule governing these two auxiliary verbs doesn't even warrant as many lines. It's easy to see why. The rule aims to distinguish between a simple future tense (*shall* for first person, *will* for second and third person) and a strong statement of intent (*will* for first person, *shall* for second and third). Obviously we are well rid of such arcane distinctions. Use whichever word sounds natural or suitable. In most cases, that will be *will*.

As for *should* and *would*, Kingsley Amis points out that *would* has been pushing out *should* even more effectively than *will* has been overcoming *shall*; he opines that within a generation or so, *I should* as the past tense for *I shall* will be as archaic as *I ween*.

> **Outdated:** I should like to come to the party.

> **Correct:** Should I wear black?

shear, sheer: The verb *shear* means to cut (*The sheep need to be sheared every spring*). The adjective *sheer* has several meanings: undiluted, pure (*sheer joy*); nearly perpendicular (*sheer cliffs*); and a diaphanous fabric.

should of: Make that *should have*.

sic (Lat., "thus"): Placed in brackets, *sic* indicates an error in an original document. It's a way of making sure the error is attributed to the one responsible for it.

> The candidate's position paper declared that one of his tenants [sic] was open government.

sight, site. See CITE.

silicon, silicone: *Silicon* is an abundant, nonmetallic element that's important in computer technology; *silicone* is a class of polymers with many properties and uses (e.g., silicone implants).

simplistic: The word suggests overlooking necessary detail, not merely simple.

> We need a comprehensive program, not just some simplistic suggestions.

sine qua non (Lat., SIN-naa kwah NOHN): The translation of this useful phrase, "without which not," has the indirection of Pennsylvania Dutch, but its meaning is clear: the essential part.

Words are the sine qua non of writing.

skimp. See SCRIMP.

soi disant (Fr., SWAH dee-SAHnt): So-called, self-styled.

soigné (Fr., swah-nyaa): Sophisticated, elegant.

sojourn: A *sojourn* is a temporary stay in one place, not the trip itself.

Wrong: I made a sojourn to Tahiti.

Right: During my sojourn in Tahiti, I learned to snorkle.

solecism: Originally a grammatical or syntactic error; now broadened to include violations of etiquette and errors in general.

Using a singular verb with *data* is no longer a solecism.

Though once viewed as a solecism, appearing hatless is now acceptable in some churches.

sotto voce (It., SOH-toh VOH-chaa "under the voice"): Spoken softly.

soupçon (Fr., soop-SOHN, "suspicion"): Small amount; a trace.

Give me just a soupçon of dessert.

specious. See FALLACIOUS.

stalemate. See IMPASSE.

stanch, staunch: Both words, which some dictionaries list as synonyms, are derived from the same word. But *stanch* and *staunch* can be usefully distinguished from each other. When you want a verb that means to stop the flow (as of blood or red ink), use *stanch*. When you want an adjective meaning loyal, steadfast, use *staunch*.

> Quick action by the government stanched the flow of capital into offshore accounts.

> She was a staunch supporter of election reform.

stationary, stationery: The word that means unmoving or fixed is *stationary*; the word that describes what you use for writing letters (remember them?) is *stationery*.

strait: A *strait* is a narrow body of water; it is the correct word to use in straitlaced and straitjacket (not "straightlaced" or "straightjacket").

stratagem, strategy: Note the difference in spelling: strategy, stratagem. A *stratagem* is a tactic designed to deceive; a *strategy* is an overall plan of attack.

> Their strategy for resolving the dispute included the stratagem of speaking with each employee even though they did not plan to take employee comments into account.

straw man: Something that is easily knocked down; thus, often used with respect to an argument.

> The straw man argument that the public is uninterested in election reform does not hold up under close scrutiny.

Spoonerisms: The question whether the Reverend William Spooner intentionally switched word beginnings ("Let me sew you to your sheet" for "Let me show you to your seat") will probably never be resolved. What is undisputed is that he started word lovers in search of similar mix-ups. Don Hauptman (author of *Cruel and Unusual Puns*) is a master of the genre; he contributed the following:

Song favored by magicians' assistants: "The First Time Ever I Faced Your Saw."

Amiable tailor: "It's a measure to pleat you."

Massage instruction: a class of touch.

Bowlers of the world, arise! You have nothing to choose but your lanes!

stubborn. See OBSTINATE.

subconscious, unconscious: *Subconscious* has a psychological connotation, indicating below the level of awareness (*probing subconscious memories*). *Unconscious* is commonly used in the general sense of unaware (*unconscious movements*).

succeed, supersede: To *succeed*, in addition to its meaning of achieving a desired objective, means to come next in succession, to replace another in office.

She succeeded in bringing all parties together for the first time.

Prince Charles is next in line to succeed Queen Elizabeth II.

Supersede (note the spelling) means to take the place of or render something obsolete.

> The new directive superseded all others.

sui generis (SOO-EE JEN-er-iss): Of its own kind, unique; used when describing a person, place, or thing that is unlike any other. Yosemite and Elvis Presley come to mind.

supine. See PRONE.

systematic, systemic: *Systematic* means orderly, methodical. *Systemic* is an adjective that means pertaining to an entire system or to the body as a whole, not just one organ.

Tt

tabula rasa (Lat.): Blank slate.

> Despite all my late-night cramming, my mind was a tabula rasa when I took the exam.

tactile, tangible. See PALPABLE.

Tom Swifties: The original adverbial form of this diversion ("I can't find the oranges," said Tom fruitlessly) has spawned a verbal variation called Croakers ("I'm dying," he croaked), as well as occupational offshoots and no doubt others. (Warning: May be habit-forming.)

take. See BRING.

tautology. See PLEONASM.

⭐**tenant, tenet:** These nouns share a Latin root (*tenere*, "to hold") but have distinct meanings. A *tenant* is someone who rents or leases property; a *tenet* is a belief or doctrine, usually of an organization.

> Shared responsibility is one of the main tenets of the tenants' association.

terra firma (Lat.): Solid ground.

terra incognita (Lat.): Unknown territory.

tête-à-tête (Fr., "head to head"): Private conversation.

⭐**than, then:** *Than* is used in statements comparing unequal elements (*I like this better than that; I'd rather be right than wrong*). It is also used in the sense of beyond (*I don't expect to read more than the first chapter*). Among the several meanings of *then* are a reference to time in the past or in the future (*I'll see you then*); the next in a sequence (*Then it was my turn*); accordingly, besides, on the other hand (*My age, then, remains a factor*).

⭐**that, which:** Your ear may be the best guide for which of these words to use. Something that sounds right probably is right. But if you want a rule, use *that* to introduce a restrictive clause (i.e., one that restricts the meaning) and use *which* to introduce a nonrestrictive clause. Examples convey this idea best.

> **Restrictive:** She is wearing the sweater that her mother gave to her.

Nonrestrictive: The sweater, which has hand-embroidered roses on it, was very expensive.

Commas, which *cut out the fat,*
Go with which, *never with* that.—Patricia O'Conner

British use tends to favor *which* in most sentence constructions.

theft. See BURGLARY.

there's: *There's,* a contraction of *there is,* should only be followed by a singular noun *(There's no exception to the rule).* When *there* is followed by a plural word, the correct wording is *there are (There are many reasons for the rule).*

tortuous, torturous: *Tortuous* means winding, circuitous, complex; when used figuratively, it suggests deviousness *(tortuous reasoning).* Use *torturous* when referring to the infliction of pain or torture *(a torturous episode).*

tour de force (Fr.): Great work, exceptional achievement.

toward, towards: The preferred usage in the United States is *toward* and in the United Kingdom, *towards;* but either is correct to indicate in the direction of.

translucent, transparent. See OPAQUE.

triptych (Gr., trip-tik, "threefold"): A painting on three panels.

troika (Russ., troy-kah): An alliance of three individuals.

trompe l'oeil (Fr., tromp-loy): To deceive the eye; e.g., columns painted on a facade.

troublesome. See PROBLEMATIC.

turbid, turgid: *Turbid* is muddy, impenetrable, having suspended sediment (*turbid river*); *turgid* is swollen or bloated; when describing language, it means overly ornate, grandiloquent (*turgid prose*).

Uu

übermensch (Ger.): Superman.

unconscious. See SUBCONSCIOUS.

More Tom Swifties

The tailor thanked his customer fittingly.

"Two plus two is four," the teacher added.

"We've taken over the government," the general cooed.

"You can't really train a beagle," he dogmatized.

"That's no beagle, it's a mongrel," she muttered.

"The fire is going out," he bellowed.

"No frankincense for me," he demurred.

"I'll never stick my fist into the lion's cage again," Tom said offhandedly.

"I'm losing my hair," Tom bawled.

unexceptional, unexceptionable: *Unexceptional* means ordinary; *unexceptionable* means above reproach, not open to objection. The words are not interchangeable.

uninterested. See DISINTERESTED.

unique: One of a kind; sole. In view of its meaning, it is inappropriate to use a qualifier such as *very* with this adjective.

use, utilize. See EMPLOY.

usufruct (Lat., YEW-zhuh-fruhkt): A noun meaning the right to use and enjoy the fruits and output of someone else's property, as long as the property isn't damaged or altered in the process. What a concept!

Vv

vade mecum (Lat., VAA-day MEE-kum, "go with me"): A reference or useful guide that one keeps at hand.

varied, various. See DIFFERENT.

vehement, violent, virulent: *Vehement* is emphatic, expressing strong emotions or convictions. *Violent* indicates strong emotions resulting in excessive force. *Virulent* is bitterly hostile, antagonistic; it also describes poisonous or pathogenic diseases, toxins, or microorganisms.

verbal. See ORAL.

 very: Don't use this adverb to prop up a weak adjective *(The meal was very good)*; instead, choose a stronger adjective *(The meal was delicious)*. Or simply omit it *(Her decision is crucial)*.

viable: This word means capable of being brought to full term (with respect to fetuses). In any other sense, strike it from your vocabulary, ". . . not for any elaborate semantic reason," as Kingsley Amis says, "but simply because it has taken the fancy of every trendy little twit on the lookout for a posh word for *feasible, practicable*."

ODDS & ENDS

Vogue Words: Overuse turns a word into a cliché, making language stale. Membership on this list fluctuates from month to month, so I suggest that you notice which words seem to be on everyone's lips and look for fresher alternatives. Here are my current candidates.

bottom line	lifestyle
charisma	matrix
constructive	meaningful
cost-effective	network (as a verb)
cutting edge	-oriented (as in
dialog	"sports-oriented")
downside/downsize	paradigm
empower	parameter
epiphany	proactive
escalate	relate
eventuate	relevant
exposure	scenario
framework	upside
identify with	viable
impact	win-win
interface	worst-case

videlicet (Lat.): That is, namely; abbreviated *viz.*

virtually. See PRACTICALLY.

vis-à-vis (Fr., vee-zah-vee): Face to face; compared with, in relation to.

vital. See PIVOTAL.

voir dire (Fr., vwar deer): To speak the truth; the process by which lawyers select a jury.

vouchsafe: A verb that means to condescend to grant a favor, a reply, or a privilege; to deign. Not many people use this word nowadays.

vox populi (Lat., "voice of the people"): Popular opinion.

waist, waste: The *waist* is the area around the middle of the torso. The noun *waste* means a ruin, trash, a thoughtless expenditure *(a waste of talent)*. The verb *waste* is to make a thoughtless expenditure *(to waste money)*, to become weak *(to waste away)*.

waive, wave: The verb to *waive* means to relinquish a claim or right voluntarily; to dispense with; to refrain from insisting upon; to put off for the time. The verb *wave* is to move up and down or back and forth in the air; to signal with the hand or an object. The noun *wave* is a ridge or swell moving along the surface of a body of water.

> *Britannia rules the waves; others waive the rules.*
> —Anonymous

waiver, waver: The noun *waiver* means the intentional relinquishing of a right or claim; the verb *waver* means to hesitate.

well. See GOOD.

weltanschauung (Ger., velt-ahn-SHAU-ung): Worldview, philosophy, especially from a specified standpoint.

weltschmerz (Ger., velt-shmairtz): World pain, weariness; a feeling of sadness that results from the evils of the world.

> When I watch the evening news, I experience a strong feeling of weltschmerz.

which. See THAT.

while: The noun *while* means a period of time. See AWHILE in "One Word or Two?", p. 29. As a conjunction, the most precise use of *while* is with reference to time *(enjoy it while you can)*. *While* is acceptable, though less well established, when it means although, whereas, or despite the fact that. Reword if there is ambiguity.

> **Wrong:** I had a childhood of comparative comfort, while my parents were forced onto the labor market early.

> **Right:** Unlike my parents, I had a childhood of comparative comfort.

who, that: Use *who* (or *whom*) when referring to a person or an animal with a name.

> Sebastian, who lives next door, borrowed my CD burner.

> Bowser, who waits for me every evening, wags his tail when he sees me.

Use *that* when referring to a family, company, country, or other entity.

The company that provides generous health-care benefits earns the loyalty of its workers.

The couple that won the lottery gave half of the money to local charities.

who, whom: Life just got simpler. I've joined the mob of language lovers who see only one use for *whom*: immediately following a preposition.

To whom shall I address my letter?

My mother, from whom I inherited my love of music, plays the piano well.

Give the book to whomever you wish.

It's important to retain this use of *whom*, for we certainly wouldn't want the inelegance of *For* Who *the Bell Tolls*. But everywhere else, it's downright liberating to abandon *whom* in favor of *who*.

Who's the letter addressed to?

Who are you imitating?

See also BETWEEN YOU AND I (ME).

Wellerisms, like malapropisms, are named after a literary character (in this case, from Dickens). How to describe them? By an example.

"That isn't the point," said the man to the would-be assassin who tried to stab him with the hilt of a dagger.

will, would. See SHALL/WILL, SHOULD/WOULD.

workable. See FEASIBLE.

worse, worst. See BETTER/BEST, WORSE/WORST.

would of: Make that *would have*.

> I would have answered sooner, but I was busy.

wreak, wreck. See REEK.

wunderkind (Ger., VOON-der-kint, "wonder child"): A prodigy.

Xx Yy Zz

X-ray: Correct with either an uppercase X or lowercase x, but always use a hyphen.

yoke, yolk: The noun *yoke* is a crossbar designed to distribute a load across someone's shoulders or to hitch together two animals; *yoke* is sometimes used as a verb (*The oxen were yoked to the plow*). The noun *yolk* is the yellow part of an egg; it's never used as a verb.

yokel: A country bumpkin.

zeitgeist (Ger., tziit-giist): Spirit of the time.

What Do They Mean When They Say . . . ?

Here are a few expressions and literary allusions, together with their explanations.

between Scylla (SIL-la) **and Charybdis** (kah-RIB-dis): Refers to those occasions when avoiding one hazard exposes one to destruction by another. Homer personified this dilemma in two female monsters who inhabited the area bounded by Scylla, a rock on the Italian side of the Strait of Messina, and Charybdis, a whirlpool on the opposite side. Similar to "between a rock and a hard place."

bowdlerize: Named after Thomas Bowdler, who published an expurgated edition of Shakespeare in the 17th century. His aim was to create a version that could be "read aloud in a family." The term is now applied to any prudish cleaning up of a literary work.

caduceus: A serpent-entwined rod that was carried by Hermes (herald and messenger of the gods); it enabled him to fly and to lull to sleep the souls of the dead before carrying them to the underworld. Now why do you suppose the medical profession would have chosen such a symbol?

Cassandra: The daughter of Priam and Hecuba, Cassandra was cursed by Apollo to foretell the truth but never be believed until it was too late. To be a Cassandra is to be a doomsayer that nobody takes seriously.

draconian: Designates a law or code of extreme severity (*draconian measures*). Named after Draco, an Athenian lawyer whose code was rigorous and harsh.

Faustian bargain: In such an agreement, you sell your soul to the devil in exchange for power or possessions, as Dr. Faustus did in Goethe's play *Faust*.

Gordian knot: A complex problem awaiting a swift, decisive resolution. Alexander provided such a resolution when, with a single stroke, he cut the intricate knot tying the wagon of Gordias to a pole; this earned him the right to rule Asia.

hoist with his own petard: Injured by his own cleverness. A *petard* is a firecracker or small, bell-shaped bomb used to breach a wall. From the French *péter*, meaning to break wind. You're on your own here.

litmus test: Any means of separating people or things into categories based on their true nature, as litmus paper distinguishes acids and bases.

Luddite: Someone who opposes technological progress; named after the 18th century movement of British workers who were fearful that machines would deprive them of jobs. The movement may have been named after Ned Lud.

Machiavellian: Niccolò Machiavelli was a 16th-century Florentine statesman whose book *The Prince* described ways to acquire and maintain power. His name has come to be identified with someone who is power-hungry and without scruple. However, Machiavelli's defenders see him as a patriotic foe of the foreign oppression that prevailed in Italy for centuries. "No great man has been so completely misunderstood," claimed T. S. Eliot. Popular usage nonetheless equates *Machiavellian* with being cunning and unscrupulous.

milquetoast: An excessively timid person; based on the comic strip character from the 1930s, Caspar Milquetoast.

Mrs. Grundy: A character (in *Speed the Plough,* an 18th-century play by Thomas Morton) who, though she never appears on stage, is evidently the village censor. Concern about "what Mrs. Grundy would think" affects the actions of some of the characters in the play. Similar to "How would it play on Main Street?"

Occam's razor: The principle that "simpler is better," which William of Occam enunciated in the 14th century. As he put it, "Entities should not be multiplied beyond what is needed."

Pandora's box: Pandora, the first woman in Greek mythology, was created as a punishment for Prometheus, who had stolen fire from heaven. She was entrusted with a box containing all the ills of humankind, but when she opened it out of curiosity, she released those ills upon the earth. The only thing she managed to prevent from escaping from the box was hope. The term is loosely used to describe a course of action that will have unknown, horrendous consequences.

Panglossian: A term used when describing someone who is indomitably optimistic (one could say terminally optimistic); named for Dr. Pangloss, a character in Voltaire's *Candide*. Dr. Pangloss's philosophy was "All is for the best in the best of possible worlds."

Pyrrhic victory: A victory that comes with staggering losses. Named after the victory of Pyrrhus over the Romans in 279 B.C., following which Pyrrhus is reputed to have said, "One more such victory, and we are lost."

Rubicon: To cross the Rubicon is to embark on an undertaking from which one cannot turn back. Caesar's crossing of the river by that name began a civil war.

serendipity: A facility for making fortunate discoveries by accident. Coined by Horace Walpole in the 18th century after the characters in the fairy tale *The Three Princes of Serendip*.

shibboleth: (1) A doctrine or principle once held to be essential by a group but now widely considered to be passé, outdated. (2) A password that reliably distinguishes one group from another. The word comes from the biblical story that describes the fatal consequences of the inability of the Ephraimites to pronounce the *sh* sound in the word *shibboleth* (Judges 12:6).

Waterloo: A decisive and final defeat. Waterloo was the Belgian town where Wellington defeated Napoleon in 1815.

Figures of Speech

Perhaps when aiming for a certain effect, you use some of the following figures of speech without knowing their fancy names.

catechresis (Gr., kaa-tuh-KREE-sis): A deliberately paradoxical choice of words.

> She would roll over in her grave if she were alive today.

hysteron proteron (Lat., HIS-tur-on PRAH-tur-on): Reversal of the natural order of ideas.

> For God, for country, and for Yale.

litotes (Gr., LIH-tuh-teez): An affirmative is expressed by negating its opposite.

> War is not healthy for children and other living things.

metonomy (Lat., meh-TAHN-nuh-mee): Using a word in such a way that it evokes a larger concept.

> The pen is mightier than the sword.

syllepsis (Lat., sil-LEP-sis): Combining a word with others that are understood differently.

> *We must all hang together or we will all hang separately.*
> —Benjamin Franklin

synecdoche (Lat., sih-NEK-duh-kee): A broader, more inclusive term replaces a less inclusive one, or vice versa.

> the law (the police)

Madison Avenue (advertising industry)

head (cattle)

tmesis (Gr., TMEE-sis): Intensifying a word or phrase by inserting one or more words in the middle of it.

West—by God—Virginia

zeugma (Gr., ZOOG-mah, "a joining or yoking"): Intentionally using a word as part of two or more constructions:

I just blew a tire and three blood vessels.

Time flies like an arrow; fruit flies like a banana.—Groucho Marx

Zeugma also covers such grammatical inconsistencies as "U.S. policy toward Lower Slobbovia has and will continue to be held hostage to demands for reparations." Make that "has been and will continue to be . . ."

Hyperbole, metaphor, and simile are also figures of speech. Their definitions are included in the A-to-Z list.

Additional Resources

The following books are ones that I found helpful while writing this book. Although some of them are now out of print, you can probably find them at a library or used-book store. For additional listings, see *Write Right!* and *Rewrite Right!*

Books

Amis, Kingsley. *The King's English: A Guide to Modern Usage*. New York: St. Martin's Press, 1997.

Augarde, Tony. *The Oxford Guide to Word Games*. New York, and Oxford, England: Oxford University Press, 1984.

Bernstein, Theodore. *The Careful Writer: A Modern Guide to English Usage*. Rockland, Maine: Free Press, 1995.

———. *Dos, Don'ts & Maybes of English Usage*. New York: Gramercy Books, 1977.

———. *Reverse Dictionary*. New York: Times Books, 1988.

Borgmann, Dmitri A. *Language on Vacation*. New York: Scribners, 1965.

Bowler, Peter. *The Superior Person's Book of Words*. Boston: David R. Godine, 1979.

Bryson, Bill. *A Dictionary of Troublesome Words*. New York: Broadway Books, 2002.

Chapman, Robert L. *Roget's International Thesaurus*, 5th ed. New York: HarperCollins, 1992.

Ibid., ed. *Roget A to Z*. New York: HarperCollins, 1994.

Ciardi, John. *Browser's Dictionary*. New York: Harper & Row, 1980.

———. *Good Words to You*. New York: Harper & Row, 1987.

———. *Second Browser's Dictionary*. New York: Harper & Row, 1983.

Dohan, Mary Helen. *Our Own Words*. New York: Knopf, 1974.

Espy, Willard R. *Another Almanac of Words at Play*. New York: Clarkson Potter, 1980.

———. *Say It My Way: How to Avoid Certain Pitfalls of Spoken English, together with a decidedly informal history of how our language rose (or fell)*. New York: Doubleday, 1980.

———. *The Word's Gotten Out*. New York: Clarkson Potter, 1989.

Fowler, H. W. *A Dictionary of Modern English Usage*, 3d rev. ed. New York, and Oxford, England: Oxford University Press, 2000.

Garner, Bryan A. *The Oxford Dictionary of American Usage and Style*. New York: Berkley Books, 2000.

King, Stephen. *On Writing: A Memoir of the Craft*. New York: Scribner, 2000.

Lederer, Richard, and Richard Dowis. *Sleeping Dogs Don't Lay*. New York: St. Martin's Press, 1999.

Lovinger, Paul W. *The Penguin Dictionary of American English Usage and Style*. New York: Penguin Reference, 2000.

Morris, Evan. *The Word Detective: Solving the Mysteries behind Those Pesky Words and Phrases*. New York: Plume Books, 2001.

Smith, Ken. *Junk English*. New York: Blast Books, 2001.

Sutcliffe, Andrea J., ed. *The New York Public Library Writer's Guide to Style and Usage*. New York: HarperCollins, 1994.

Periodicals

Verbatim: The Language Quarterly
(800) 897-3006
Mailing address: 4907 N. Washington Ave., Chicago, IL 60625

The Vocabula Review
Website: www.vocabula.com
(781) 861-1515
Mailing address: 10 Grant Place, Lexington, MA 02420

Word Ways: The Journal of Recreational Linguistics (quarterly)
Email: wordways@juno.com
Website: www.wordways.com
Mailing address: Spring Valley Road, Morristown, NJ 07960

Websites

About two dozen websites are listed in *Write Right!*, but you'll probably be able to find everything you want at just one of them. Richard Lederer's **www.verbivore.com** includes such links as following:

- etymology

- grammar and usage

- language columns and online magazines

- language reference links (American Slanguages, Cliché Finder)

- linguistic links

- newsgroups (anagram afficionados, punsters, and others)

- reference (dictionaries and thesauri)

- word games and word play

- word watching and vocabulary development

Best of all, Lederer keeps it all up to date.

Acknowledgments

My indebtedness to others in creating what is now five books has reached a critical mass. It's time to acknowledge in print some of the help I've received over the years.

Pat Ditzler, Betty Jane Darling, Phyllis McCreery, Joyce Cass, and Janet Harms have been willing guinea pigs, patiently reading through rough drafts, giving me feedback, and providing some of the best examples in the book. Suzanne Byerley's critiques always added professional polish.

Every writer should be so lucky as to have a daughter like Carol to help with shaping a book. Carol's talent for finding weak points and suggesting remedies contributed mightily to this book and to all the others.

My husband, Wayne, has been a willing technical editor, ensuring accuracy when the text touched on matters of science or math. His careful approach also caught inconsistencies that had slipped by everyone else.

A glance through these pages suggests the importance of Andrea Penn's drawings in the final product. What it doesn't reveal is that she sometimes provided text as well (see the *its/it's* example). This was typical of her above-and-beyond style.

Of the numerous editors I've had in twenty years at Ten Speed Press, Kathy Hashimoto is one of the best. She knows just where to give me free rein and where to tug me back to the real world. Her enthusiasm has been essential in bringing together the elements that create a successful book.

My thanks to all!

Index

The words and phrases that constitute most of *The Right Word!* are listed alphabetically in Tricky Words and Handy Phrases. They are not duplicated here.

Also from Jan Venolia

5³/₈ x 7 inches
200 pages

5³/₈ x 7 inches
224 pages

6 x 9 inches
128 pages

*Available from your local bookstore, or by ordering direct
from the publisher. Write for our catalogs of over
1,000 books and posters.*

TEN SPEED PRESS
Celestial Arts / Tricycle Press

P.O. Box 7123, Berkeley, CA 94707
www.tenspeed.com
800-841-2665 or fax 510-559-1629
order@tenspeed.com